For Joe Matis
and David Cunningham

# THE TALL BOY

**Jess Gregg**

with a lot of happy
memories of you guys.
Jess Gregg –

the permanent press
sag harbor, new york

August, 2005

**Library of Congress Cataloging-in-Publication Data**

Gregg, Jess-
The tall boy: memoir / by Jess Gregg
p. cm.
ISBN 1-57962-119-8 (alk. paper)
1. Gregg, Jess - - Home and hunts- -California- -Los Angeles (Calif.)- -Social life and customs. 3. Authors, American- -20th century- -Biography. 4. Gay youth- -California- -Los Angeles. 5. Gay men- -United States- -Biography. 6. Gregg, Jess- -Friends and associates. 7. Gregg, Jess- -Childhood and youth. I. Title

PS3557.R432Z476 2005
813'.54- -dc22
[B]

2005045838



Printed in The United States of America

THE PERMANENT PRESS
4170 Noyac Road
Sag Harbor, NY 11963

*For Marijane Meaker*
*and the bunch at Ashawagh Hall*

**By Jess Gregg**

**Novels**

The Other Elizabeth
The Glory Circuit
Baby Boy

**Plays**

The Seashell
Shout from the Rooftops
Cowboy
The Mens Room
The Undergound Kite

# - 1 -

## FEBRUARY, 1943

Hollywood Boulevard was crowded, but nobody seemed to be going anywhere. The tourists drifted aimlessly, and so did I, until I noticed that one of them was cruising me. To make certain, I slowed my pace, finally pausing to glance in a shop window. He stopped too, and I could see the reflection of his smile in the plate glass. He was a few years older than I, in his late twenties perhaps, and more solidly built. With his fresh complexion and new sports shirt, he looked like a recently demobilized sailor getting his first gape at Glitter Gulch.

"What's doin'?" he asked.

"Nothing much," I told him. "Just heading home."

There was something lazy in his smile. "Live around here?"

I shook my head. "Live with my folks."

Lazy, even intimate: "If you got wheels, we could always drive out to the beach—-"

The suggestion was not irresistible. At twenty-two, I was choosy, and he wasn't really my type. However, I was a little tight, he was ready, and, anyway, why not? We strolled down a dark side street to where I was parked, and got into my car. As I turned the key in the ignition, he sprawled back slightly in the seat.

"Oh, man, I'm bustin' my jeans," he laughed. The knee he pressed against mine invited me to find out.

I did, and the fact was, he had considerably overstated his condition. Still, I let out the brake, and we pulled away from the curb. At the first boulevard stop, he said curtly, "Turn left!" Surprised at his tone, I glanced at him. He was holding his wallet open to a glint of brass. Whatever else he said was drowned out by the booming realization that I was under arrest.

Stunned, suddenly sober, I followed his directions and

drove several blocks deeper into the night. Thoroughly business-like now, he told me to stop in front of a squat, modestly-lit municipal building. Here, we were joined by an unmarked car, which apparently had been following us—decoy cops, like nuns, travel in twos. They went through my pockets, patted their hands under my arms and down my thighs, then searched my car with the same close attention. Nothing incriminating was found, although the glove compartment produced a snapshot of a girl I had dated in college. "Is this a guy in drag?" the second officer asked.

After my car had been impounded and the keys taken, the detective marched me into the station house. A policeman at the front desk greeted him cheerfully. "You pull in *another* fag?"

"Yep," said my detective, grinning modestly.

"Guess it takes one to know one," the desk man teased.

I was left alone in an empty back room. The bleak glare of the fluorescent tubes on the ceiling drained the color from everything but the black fur on the ventilator grill. I paced back and forth, trying to jump-start my brain. What I would say or how I would explain, I had no idea. I had never been arrested before. Nor had I spent much time weighing the cause or consequence of my sexuality—had simply accepted what had been dealt to me, same as I did with being tall, or having no gift for algebra. Since my actions weren't motivated by malice or greed, they didn't seem any more criminal to me than the instinct that Sally and Joe celebrate in some lovers' lane.

This view, however, was not shared by the dumpy plainclothesman who shortly came in. He sat down opposite me and laconically put his questions, while the husky young decoy copied down my replies. I answered straightforwardly, probably following the rule of behavior set since childhood: if you were truthful and cooperative, you would be forgiven.

But childhood was far away now. I was driven downtown to the seedy commercial district, where the white finger of City Hall marked the police headquarters. As I was taken inside, the decoy cop suddenly became chatty, especially about his wife. It was as if he had to make scrupulously clear to me, or even to himself, that he had only been playing a part on Hollywood Boulevard. "No hard feelings," he added, marching me along a corridor. "It's just my job."

Still trying to understand, I asked, "Then who have I harmed?"

Evidently he had been asked this question before, because he didn't pause to think before answering. "Just that we can't allow this kind of thing to go on," he said.

It was all the answer I was to get. In mid-twentieth century America, all questions about this matter had been satisfactorily taken care of by pulling down poor old Oscar Wilde some fifty years earlier. Although a smirk was permissible, nice people didn't mention homosexuality. Both law and religion regarded it as a kind of willfulness that only tar and feathers could cure. Movies forbad any hint of it, and if novels highlighted the subject, they were likely not to be reviewed or advertised by decent newspapers Regarded as criminal or sick, and with imprisonment always a threat, the gay world was necessarily a secret society, with its own private vocabulary, but no political voice. If one survived in this mine field, it was thanks to guts, intuition, and humor. And luck.

But luck seemed to have run out on me when I was shortly booked on a lewd vagrancy charge, and hurriedly fingerprinted. Too hurriedly, it seems, and by an apparent rookie, for a few minutes later the whole agonizing process had to be done over correctly, each finger pressed in ink and individually rolled from side to side on the printed form. A junkie, waiting in line behind me, asked if this was "my first time in the slam?" Someone told him to shut up, and he dodged involuntarily as if to avoid a fist. A moment later, he was whispering again, advising me not to let them see that I cared. The phrase he used should have made me smile, considering my already conspicuous height. "Walk tall," he said.

Neither pride nor poise was equal to the storm inside me, however, and in an effort to quiet it, I began blocking out each impression as it happened—a kind of self-hypnosis I had experimented with before in the dentist's chair. As a result, I have no clear picture of what happened next. I don't think I was locked in the tank with the drunks and vagrants, nor was I taken into night court; yet my dread of both possibilities left an impression so vivid, it passes today as memory. All I can be sure of is that, some time between midnight and forever, I was handed a yellow phone book and told to choose someone to stand my bail.

There were pages and pages devoted to this service—*open all night,* most of them read, and some, *next door to the jail.* Soon I was filling out a bond agreement with a sullen middle-aged man in a too-sharp suit. When I was released, he consented to taxi me to my father's house for an additional seventy-five dollars. His silent contempt as we sped through the deserted streets, however, was gratis.

When we reached home, I ran inside and scraped together whatever money I could find, some of it in nickels and dimes, and brought this back to the car. The bond man counted it carefully, and then as I turned to go, said, "Wait!" I glanced back. His eyes were still contemptuous, but furtively he ran his hand down the inside of his leg. "How about it?" he asked. I did not reply, but crossed the lawn and let myself back into the house.

No one was awake. Tiptoeing up to my room, I stripped quickly and got into the shower, compulsively scrubbing myself as if the disinfectant smell of jail were still clinging to me. What little perspective remained had to battle an impulse to destroy the clothes I had worn that night. Shirt, slacks, and shorts finally went into the laundry hamper, and my tweed jacket to the back of my closet. As far as I know, I never wore it again.

It was nearly four in the morning, but there was no hope of sleep. Some time in the next twenty-four hours, I was due to face a magistrate, and it was already clear to me that, for the first time in my life, I was entirely on my own. The advice I had always gotten from my father, and the emotional support from my mother, were suddenly out of reach—I had misery enough without causing theirs. Yet costs had already accumulated that I could not take care of alone.

Forcing myself to sit down, I tried to take stock of my resources. I had a Swiss watch I could sell, and a car that I could not—my family would ask questions if it disappeared. In my last year at college, I had begun to sell some of my stories to the magazines, but income from this was modest and only occasional. Living at home, I had been able to save a little money, yet the grand total of my assets fell far short of what I was going to need. Still less encouraging was the list of people I could turn to for help. At most, there were two, and neither would thank me for waking them up before daylight.

Sitting down by the telephone, I tried to relax while waiting for morning to come. A quote I couldn't identify, maybe from the Bible, maybe Shakespeare, kept echoing through my head: *The gods are just, and of our pleasant vices make instruments to scourge us.* I couldn't sleep, and yet sometimes a dream slipped between my eye and reality, a sort of delusive contact lens that simultaneously clarified and obscured who I was, and the mess I was in. Trying to fix the blame for what had happened to me tonight only made things worse, yet there was relief, almost rest, in some of the involuntary visions of myself as I had been: Jess, short for Jesse, named for my grandfather, called "Bud" at home, and "the tall boy" by my teachers at school—

## - 2 -

## BIG PAL

I was shooting up too fast—at eleven, was nearly as tall as my father, and towered over everyone else in my class at school. The trouble was, I didn't weigh any more than before. During an examination, our family doctor asked if I played with myself. "Most of the time," I told him. His glance seemed odd, and I explained that there were no other kids in the neighborhood, so naturally I played alone.

He got kind of brisk, and pointed out the difference between playing *by* myself and *with* myself. Apparently both were frowned upon, but at least he had an immediate remedy for the solitude: "Get him out in the world," he advised my mother and father. "Have him meet people, help him make friends, the boy's growing up lonely and out-of-step."

It had never occurred to me that I was either one. I had a great dog, a terrier, who practically understood English. And even when he was busy elsewhere, I had books to read—-Poe, Dickens, even kid stuff like the Oz books. My life teemed with the activities I imagined or borrowed from the movies. Still, to please my parents, I began acting like someone else, and tried attaching myself to other classmates at school. Touch football and Scout activities soon bored me, however, and my attention kept drifting back to people more my style—-Robin Hood, John Barrymore, or Marie Antoinette. It was a select group, and shortly after my twelfth birthday, it was joined by Mazie Janoski.

I met her only once, and wouldn't have met her at all, except for my mother's shameless Uncle Ike. He smoked his cigars down too far, and his neckties seemed about to spontaneously combust; but no man could be all bad who owned so many books about the circus. My sister Sharlie thought his stories about the days when he owned a traveling dog-and-pony show were tiresome, but I couldn't hear them often enough. Which is why, when the Sells-Floto Circus came to Los Angeles that spring, he invited me and not her to go see it happen "from the ground up."

He drove by for me at six in the morning, and we reached the exposition grounds in time to see men and elephants heaving the gray canvas up against the sky. We had breakfast with the roustabouts, and lunch with the performers, many of whom Uncle Ike knew. I met Irene, Queen of Escape, who climbed ladders of razor-sharp swords in her bare feet; shook hands with

Poodles Hanneford, the equestrian clown, and watched him warm up, stumbling on and off horses as if it was all a hilarious mistake. Yet even this lacked that feeling of spotlight-and-drum roll which happened when I saw the fat lady.

She was young, pretty, and for all her vast pink poundage, remarkably light on her feet. To the blare of a three-piece band, she daintily whirled and twirled, crooking out her rouged little finger; did a high kick, and sank down resoundingly in the splits. Fascinated, I dragged Uncle Ike back to the sideshow three times to watch her perform. Even when her act was over, and the crowd passed along to gape at the Armless Wonder, I kept watching her. She was dressed as a child, her pink costume short and beltless, with a butterfly bow perched in her baby curls. Most heavy women sit clumsily, their legs spread apart, as if playing an unseen cello, but this one crossed her ankles like a young lady, demurely fanning herself with a pleat of newspaper. The second time she caught me watching, she smiled and beckoned. For once, no shyness held me back. By stretching up on tiptoe, I could rest my chin on her platform, and she leaned forward in her reinforced chair. "What's your name, little pal?" she asked.

I began to say Buddy, then changed it to Jess, and it came out Bus.

Somehow she understood and told me she had two names too—her real name, Mazie Janoski, and her billing. She waved at the weathered canvas banner that identified her as Jolly Dolly, the Dancing Fat Girl. "But they already had that painted before I even joined the show," she explained.

She chatted on in faintly accented speech, from time to time winking reassuringly at Uncle Ike. Once she interrupted herself to ask, "Bet you could eat some cotton candy, Buddy, huh?"

I had a quarter in my pocket, and said, with the gallantry I had learned from Sydney Carton in *A Tale of Two Cities,* "I'd rather buy some for you."

She showed her dimples, an improbable galaxy of them. "You be my guest today," she said, and flagged a white-aproned vendor. "I can't eat that spun stuff no how," she added. "Makes me sick, and then I lose weight. I'm already too light for this job."

I glanced again at her poster, which boasted that she weighed a thousand pounds. She rolled her eyes up and giggled. "Never been more than five hundred," she confided, "and sometimes only four eighty-five." She leaned closer, and I could feel the moist warmth she radiated. "Your mama's worried about your weight, ain't that so, little pal?" She reached out and smoothed my hair with her pleated fan. "Oh, I'd fatten you up if you was my boy. I'd put the roses in your cheeks."

Did she really say that? I'm not sure, for by the following day, I had gone over our conversation a hundred times, and with each repetition, changed it for the better. Did she actually ask Uncle Ike to bring me back after the big show and eat dinner with her? I don't think so. Had I promised to write her a letter? Maybe not, but it was a marvelous idea, and I began composing it in my head almost at once.

Several days passed before it was ready to be set down on paper. I used my father's best stationery, although not enough was going on in my life to justify three pages. The snapshot I included was to help her remember who I was. Not until the envelope was sealed did I face the fact that I didn't know where to send it: Circuses don't wait around like houses do. Nonetheless, I included everything I knew in the address—her real name, her billing, the sideshow, the name of the circus, the city, the state—and, printing *Please Forward* under all this, left it to the Post Office to earn the three cents I invested in stamps. I did not hold my breath or do anything silly like classmates who had written fan letters to movie stars—after all, this was someone I *knew*—but I awoke each morning with a thrilling sense that this might be The Day. For a week, it wasn't. Then the mailman dropped a pink envelope into our door slot. It was postmarked San Francisco, and there was a Mr. in front of my name just as if I were grown up.

Her letter was written with a soft lead pencil, and while this has faded over the years, it is still legible. "Dear Little pal Budy," it reads. "You dear and most welcome letter this A.M. and was I surprise. Yes I do Rember you and all redy have the picture of you on my mirrer and look at quite offen. My nephew graduate from 8 grade at 15 year old his huby is foot ball. I gave him a gold football for Chrismas present. My Mother gave rest watch he is on the oner row. We are prode of him. Dearest pal you mus study hard and make you grades every year so can graduate to. Rember I bet on you & hope you all luck a pal could wish a nother. Well Buddy I gess I have tolde all the new for this time hope to have letter soon again & send a nother snap shot of you if you have one to spear. Love from Big pal Mazie."

It is a comment on my sixth grade education that I noticed nothing wrong with her spelling. What I did notice was something in myself. I could not quite identify it, but something seemed to fall into place and began to make sense of everything. Whatever it was, I wanted more of it, and immediately wrote to her again. She replied by return mail.

My mother and father were aware of the correspondence, but I did not want to discuss it with them. I found a hiding place for Mazie's letters in a carved Swiss chair where a large music box mechanism had been positioned. By year's end, the cavity was full. In re-reading the letters that have survived, I am struck by how alike they are. The same words keep recurring. "Little pal," "Big pal," "Study hard," "Graduate." Her concern with weight was constant, although the spelling of the word varies from sentence to sentence. ("I am glad you are Getting taul, you have plenty hight now to way 140 pouns and not be Overweght eather.") Her own health was referred to only once or twice, even when she took sick and was forced to leave the show. The letters from her mother's home in San Antonio during the ten months of recuperation iterate over and over her yearning to get back to the sideshow, as well as her expectation of our eventual reunion. ("I let you no when I go back to Circus, and when it come west we will meat—" "We will meet—" "We will see each other agen—")

Sameness made change more visible as it gradually happened. I started signing my letters Jess, sometimes adding my middle initial as my father did. And in an effort to add interest to my letters, I began to enlarge my peek-hole on the world—-experimentally went out for track after school, tried out for plays, was campaign manager for a boy who ran for class president. He did not win. "But never mind," Mazie comforted. "Don't take it personal."

She too was changing. Her spelling became a little less inventive, the handwriting considerably less intricate, and there was often punctuation. "I see how words are written in your letters," she told me, "and find them again in the newspaper. Maybe I will try a book nex. What book do you read, Buddy?" The fact is, I was halfway through a two-ton adult novel, *Anthony Adverse,* but I replied, and honestly, that I still enjoyed *The Wind in the Willows*. At Christmas, I sent her my copy. Whether she actually read it through, or just identified with the pictures I cannot guarantee, but sometimes she interrupted her news to exclaim, pertinent to nothing, "O that Mr Toad. He is just Like my whole life."

Shortly before summer, the postmark on her letter changed dramatically—

Kansas City! She had finally resumed touring with the circus. It was a small outfit, one that only played the Midwest and upper South, but her joy, at least, was three-ring. I sent her my congratulations, but apparently blundered in asking what the new freak show was like. Her reply, when it eventually arrived, was written in ink, and the absence of crossed-out words suggested it had been diligently worked over, then re-copied. "Dear Jess," she wrote, "you are sweetest boy, like my own to me, and I know you wood not hurt no one, but that is a word we never use. To ourselves we are not freaks. We are not little man or fat girl or beard lady, but only people like every one else with job to do and mother to support and dear friend to right letters to."

The letters continued until I was fifteen. My parents had sent me off to prep school in the North, and while I wrote Mazie about my class activities, I did not mention how restless I was there. The discipline was little short of martial law, and the boys, unlike myself, were earnestly conformist. Fortunately, I was not the only one singled out for their criticism. The boy in the room next to mine was from the Bahamas, the son of a wealthy planter. Blond, with an arrowhead taper to his torso, Erich showed a skill at water sports which should have guaranteed his popularity. He made no effort to fit in, however, and since uniformity was their law, the other boys gradually dropped him. This troubled him very little, but gave me a wonderful opportunity to be his only friend. I could scarcely believe my good fortune. When I'd tap on the wall at night, he'd tap back. Some mornings, we would cut class and hitch to the nearby town. Often, we did our homework together, although more often study gave way to confidences. Only a year older than I was in time, he was decades my senior in experience. He had already traveled to Europe and China. He kept a bottle of white wine under his bed. He had been with women. A blonde in Panama had called him a dollar-head. A *dollar-head?* "What's that mean?" I demanded.

He just laughed. "I'll tell you when you grow up."

I had nothing exceptional to confide in return, except my correspondence with Mazie. I had never discussed this with anyone, but to compete in his league, I finally worked it into one of our bull sessions. He listened as much as he ever listened to anyone, and then, as if I had never spoken, began recounting how he had seduced a thirty-year-old divorcee at Waikiki.

His description was graphic, and, not unaccountably, both of us got aroused. "Did she call you a dollar-head too?" I wanted to know.

"They all do," he said.

The fury of inexperience suddenly swept over me. "You made that up!" I accused. "Dollar-head, for gosh sake! There's probably no such thing!"

He marched to the door and jammed a pencil between the knob and bolt, the classic way to insure that no prowling master would burst in. Then, turning back, he opened his pajamas and showed me. I saw at once what the blonde from Panama must have meant, but was not about to inflate his already considerable pride by admitting it. "That's nothing special," I scoffed. "Everyone's got a dollar-head."

"The hell they do!" he cried.

A moment later, we were comparing notes. Trying not to breathe hard, we stood there in undetermined expectation. My mouth was so dry, my smile became beached on my teeth. "Get me hot, Jesse," he whispered abruptly, and pushed my head.

I resisted, he persisted, and we wrestled around the room, bumping into the furniture, tipping over the chairs. As I recall, we ended up in an ingenious position that so simultaneously obliged both contenders, that I was surprised nobody had ever thought of it before. When we finally opened the door again, the tension was gone, and he nudged my ribs slyly. "No wonder you write to the fat lady," he whispered. "You're a freak yourself."

"Look who's talking!" I said, and we laughed. Yet that word, freak, followed me back to my room, and I had the feeling it had been following me all my life. Why else had I sought out Mazie in the first place, if not to lull, with like company, that fear of being different?

But that defense only seemed to make me impatient now. The difference I had sensed about myself so long ago had just been proved true, and the world had not ended. I felt suddenly as if I had just graduated.

In the week that followed, I became so engrossed in self-discovery, that when a letter from Mazie arrived, I didn't immediately get around to reading it. When I did, every line of it was predictable: the admonition, the fondness, the faith. It was like being offered a second helping when I was already full. Always before, I had replied to her letters quickly, spontaneously, but this time I ran out of words after the first paragraph.

Two or three times, I was tempted to wad up my reply, and chuck it at the wastebasket. Still I kept trying to write it.

Ultimately, it lay on my desk for two more weeks. Re-reading it then, I realized there was nothing to do but let go gracefully. By some intuition, I knew that only a cad tells a woman good-bye. A gentleman says "I will never forget you." That's what I wrote at the end of my letter, and signed it the way I used to before I grew up: little pal. Then I mailed it, and ran along to the pool where Erich was waiting to teach me to swim underwater.

## - 3 -

## DRESS-UP

That was the beginning of my life. Or at least, the life that was to occupy me for years to come. My more conventional beginning had been in my grandparents' house in St. Paul. As soon as my mother and I could travel, my father brought us back home to Los Angeles; but every summer until I was nine, we returned to the Midwest. This was called "going back East", and was a terrible trial to my sister Sharlie, and consequently, me.

Her name was really Charlotte, and she was so constantly my companion, that for my first few years, I thought we were the same person. Even after I discovered we weren't, I kept wishing we were. People smiled at me tolerantly, but they *exclaimed* about her! She was very pretty with her thick tawny hair and green eyes. And though she was only fifteen months older than I, she was already wise and experienced. Before she could even talk, she had won a Beautiful Baby contest. By the time I entered kindergarten, she was already reading, and could count forever, or at least until people implored her to stop.

Best of all, she played dress-up. She needed no more than bedclothes—could drape sheets into togas, such as people

*with Sharlie in St. Paul*

wore in our favorite movie, *Ben-Hur,* or clutch the down quilt around her so that it practically duplicated the velvet wrap our mother wore to the theatre. Sharlie could convert anything into fun or adventure, which was fortunate because neither was provided in St. Paul.

There was nothing to do in that great gloomy house. Grandpa told us jokes sometimes, but Grandma was always rather formal. She didn't like us to race in the hall, and shouting was forbidden. Our mother tried to keep us entertained with jigsaw puzzles and picture books, while Effie, who had been Grandma's maid for thirty years, often took us out for walks. Not even that on Sundays, however. In California, we would have been taken to a movie or the beach, but St. Paul still observed a puritan Sabbath, a day set aside for inner research, and if possible, self-reproach. In my eyes, Sunday back East was no credit to the Creator. At least not until the Sunday Sharlie discovered the attic.

For want of something better to do, she had followed our father up the steep steps to the third floor. Naturally, I tagged along. It was a part of the house I hadn't even suspected. Shadows were deep and stationary here, lending mystery to the dusty furniture and steamer trunks. I had never been in a real attic before—in Los Angeles, we had a crawl space—and the warm, evocative smell of camphor and rose sachet hooked me at once and forever.

My father was packing away a khaki uniform and a stack of letters, when suddenly Sharlie pointed to something pink in the trunk. "What's that?"

He lifted out a pair of little old-fashioned shoes. High-heeled and satin, they were the color my mouth turned after sucking cherry drops. The heels flared out at the bottom, and the pointed toes were embroidered with tiny pearls. Sharlie held one of the shoes alongside her foot. It made her child-size look gross. Incredulous, she asked, "Who wore these?"

"No one," my father said. "They were just samples." He pointed to the shoemaker's name stamped in lacy gold letters on the inner sole. "Your grandmother used to order her shoes from Paris, and these were probably sent over to tempt her."

"Did she get tempted?"

The mere idea made him laugh: his mother was *very* correct. Returning the little shoes to the trunk, he locked it, and put the key back in an old leather pocketbook full of other keys. "Let's go downstairs now. Watch out, it's steep!"

Sharlie was unusually quiet when Effie put us down for our much-hated nap, but the minute we were alone, she was out of bed. "Quick!" she whispered. As she tiptoed out into the hall, I noticed she had the key purse looped over her arm. I followed her to the attic door, which she unlocked and held open for me.

"Why are we going up there again?" I demanded.

She seemed surprised that I even had to ask. "I'm going to try on those pink shoes," she said.

Cinderella's sisters couldn't have struggled more gamely with the glass slipper. Sharlie's feet were narrow, but even when she eventually managed to squeeze in her toes and the ball of her foot, the little satin shoe ended under her arch, leaving an inch of her heel sticking out. Since only the front view mattered anyway, she finally crushed her feet down upon the heel cups, flattening them into mules, and so was able to hobble around the attic with that clack-clack sound which is the very heartbeat of dress-up.

I paid little attention to this agonizing triumph until she suddenly emerged from the shadows. "Look at me!" she cried. The green felt hat she had perched on her thick fair hair was clearly Grandma's, although the rakish tilt was all her own. With piercing eyes and a regal toss of her head, she snapped out an order. "*Apologize to me!*"

I shouted with laughter. She sounded just like our grandmother at my seventh birthday party. Grandma had given me some toy which Sharlie had hoped was to be hers. She had expressed her disappointment a bit too impulsively—had in fact, called our stiff-necked grandmother a darn fool—and the party was suddenly over. For sheer consequence, that had been a moment in our lives second only to being born; but it made splendid drama for us now. We spent the rest of the afternoon acting out scenes in which Grandma (Sharlie) exacted apologies from a series of passersby who broke dishes and fell down and did other humorous things (me.)

This useful story line expanded astonishingly in the days that followed. The plays we composed for ourselves were full of peril, and the dialogue was largely mutual instruction. "—and then you must say that the house is on fire, and I must say, 'Quick, jump out the window,' and you must say—" Repetition gradually built these scenes into resounding climaxes. "*Help, help*," Sharlie cried, clutching her throat in terror. "*The room is full of tigers!*"

In search of inspiration, we ransacked every suitcase, chest, and packing box in the attic. However, the biggest wardrobe trunk, plastered with peeling stickers from European hotels, resisted every key in the leather purse. As a last resort, we pried open its lock with Effie's scissors. Our expectations were only moderate, and even these plunged when we lifted the lid on a full inventory of long woolen underwear. At the bottom of the trunk, however, we came upon some bundles wrapped in newspapers so old and brittle, they seemed to break apart as we opened them. "Lookit," Sharlie breathed out, bringing the contents nearer the light. "Just look at these clothes!"

They seemed to have been made for a princess. The hat, big around as a bird bath, spilled over with pink plumage. And the dress was long and silvery, sewn with tiny disks like fingernails, except glittering. "But who did these belong to?" Sharlie cried.

Certainly not our grandmother, a woman so conservative, she wore her beautiful pearls hidden unseen inside her dress. Sharlie, far more daring, was already wriggling into the quicksilver gown. The gap in back didn't show, once she put on the opera cape. This was silk so stiff it whispered when she walked—lavender, with purple chestnut leaves stitched flat around the sweeping hem. The only problem was that such grandeur so completely overwhelmed our make-believe, we could think of no drama to equal it.

This, however, was the kind of problem my sister was born to grapple with. Under her direction, war was abruptly declared, and we divided up the khaki uniform between the combative armies. Steamer trunks were lined up as barricades, and from behind these, we fired salvo after salvo at the other, each of us dying many times, though at no cost to our enjoyment. At the height of this carnage, there was an inexplicable instant of silence, as piercing as a ray of light, and into the no-man's-land stepped a princess, Sharlie in the plumed hat and glittering dress. The very incarnation of Reason, she raised one hand, and her voice was many things: entreaty, command, seduction. "War, stop!" she said. So astonishing was this idea, so unheard of, so logical, that both sides cast down their weapons. It was magnificent, of course, but there was no way to top it, so we performed it all over again.

The fourth time we repeated it, my enthusiasm was a little forced. I didn't want to cheer Sharlie's heroism anymore. I wanted some of those cheers myself. I was tired of wearing that old khaki uniform, while she got all the flash. I wanted to be the one everybody was looking at. I wanted to be the princess. "You can't be," Sharlie said, firmly. "You're a boy!"

As she had never used that argument when our limited casting had me playing the stepmothers and ugly sisters, I paid no attention. Grabbing the great feathered hat, and throwing the lavender cloak around me, I stepped out into the crossfire, and showed her how heroism was *really* done.There were no cheers, however. Instead, the hostilities intensified. Sharlie's brows were bunched, and she cried, "You just look silly like that!"

"I do not," I defended.

"You do too, you ought to see yourself!"

Actually, this was something I already had in mind, and with my finery dragging behind me, I marched downstairs toward my mother's room, where the big three-way mirror would settle any dispute about looking silly. Sharlie followed, but as we hastened across the hall, we came face to face with our grandfather.

Usually, we weren't shy with him, but now the eyes behind his glasses were troubled, and we backed away from them. "No," he said. "No, that won't do at all, sir! Get those things off!"

It was not the kind of voice that told jokes. It was the same sharp voice Grandma had used when she said, "Apologize to me!" Yet when Grandma, herself, came out of her room to see what was wrong, her voice was unexpectedly gentle. "It's too warm to play this way," she told me, and took the big hat off my head, the lavender cape from my shoulders.

Leading Sharlie and me downstairs to the music room, she got the jigsaw puzzles out for us. I wondered what I had done wrong, but her face gave me no clue. When my father came home, however, I could hear Grandpa's voice, even though he was several rooms away. "What are you raising the boy to be?" he was demanding. "Letting him play with girls all the time! Dressed-up and parading around like I don't know what! The Queen of Sheba, or—Cleo de Merode, or someone!"

"Who's Cleo de Merode?" Sharlie whispered.

Grandma did not hear. "Work your jigsaw puzzle, dear," she said.

Sharlie obeyed, but touched her toe to my shin under the card table, a way of telling me we would go right on with our dress-up the next day.

Yet the following afternoon, we found the door to the attic would no longer open. Even as we rattled the knob, we saw the metal hasp that had been newly screwed into the woodwork, and the shiny brass padlock holding it shut. We scurried around, looking for the key, even giving Effie's room a quick search. It was not there, and not in the leather purse either. Nor did it turn up anywhere else in the remaining days of our visit to St. Paul.

When we returned to Los Angeles at the end of the summer, the consequences were immediate and far-reaching. Three times a week, I was taken to a junior gymnasium after school,

Cleo de Merode

where I joined a group of young boys being drilled in swimming, calisthenics, and boxing. On Saturday nights, my father took me to basketball or hockey games, sometimes even to watch two pugs slug it out, often with sudden shows of blood. It did not interest me particularly, but I learned that ice cream was the standard reward on nights when I faked some enthusiasm.

This process, I later discovered, was called "butching up the act," and as I grew older, I was additionally packed off to a summer camp in the High Sierras every August. Here, with a swarm of other adolescent boys, I learned to rough it. We lived in tents, swam in icy water, gutted the fish we caught, and gave near-religious heed to baseball. Once I understood that my piteous letters to my parents were not going to rescue me from this, I settled down and pretended to fit in. Not all of it was time wasted. I learned most of the popular obscenities, smoked my first cigarette, heard about rubber things called "merry widows," and marveled at the inventiveness of a lout from a rival tent who exuberantly marched around with his baseball cap hung on what he called a "boner." By the end of each summer, I had acquired a deep tan, gained a few pounds, and won the kind of award that everyone else won too—improvement in riding, progress in marksmanship, headway in diving. And all this time, it was clear to me that pretending to be a regular feller was just another kind of dress-up.

This masquerade fooled some people. It seemed to fool mother and dad and my grandparents, anyway. Whether it fooled Sharlie, I had no way of knowing. She seemed to have simply vanished from my life. We had not been forbidden to play together, but she did not seem to want to, anyway. I could not be sure she was even aware of me. When I was being funny, she would appear not to notice. Even when we sat side by side in the back seat of the car, she seemed to be going in some other direction, and at a different speed. "She's growing up, dear," my mother explained.

Whatever she was doing, I wanted her to stop it. I waited

for several years for her to come back, and when she didn't, I switched my affection to Noo, a more recently born sister. Sharlie accepted this without protest. She wasn't even Sharlie anymore: her friends at school called her Sharrie, eventually Sherry. What I called her was something else, "stuck-up" being a regular instance. Other words that rushed to my mouth seemed to have been waiting there forever. "She thinks she's the Queen of Sheba," I complained to my father. "Parades around like Cleo de whatsername."

"Well, that's not so bad," my father said. "Cleo de Merode was considered the most beautiful woman in Europe when I was a boy."

He kept on talking calmly, as he often did to head off these quarrels—told us about seeing this Cleo dance at a theatre, when his parents had taken him to the Paris Exposition of 1900. "I probably wouldn't even remember," he added, "except that my mother was so disapproving."

My sister pretended to be interested, as an excuse for ignoring me. "Why did she disapprove?"

"Well, Mlle. de Merode was the King of Belgium's—" He fumbled discreetly "—best friend. She looked like a madonna, though. Great gentle eyes. But she painted them with kohl. And while all the other women piled their hair up in great puffs, she set a style by drawing hers down over her ears and knotting it at the nape of her neck. People said she hid her ears that way because the King had bitten them off."

He considered the statement. "He probably hadn't," he added. In the same inconsequential manner, he turned back to his reading. "So see if you two can't make up with each other now. All right?"

But we didn't even try. I became more expert at needling Sharlie, and several times even managed to pierce her reserve. Once when I was fourteen, she reacted with such chill indignation, I suddenly recognized its source. "*Apologize to me!*" I cried out gleefully, and she certified my hunch with a quick rush of blood to her face.

It was Grandma Gregg she was taking after, beyond any doubt—the same self-containment, the same cool glance, the same austere taste. My mother had come to this conclusion too. "But underneath her reserve, Sharlie feels very deeply," she said protectively. "Like all those women did."

"All what women?"

"Your grandmother. And *her* grandmother. The women in your father's family that Sharlie takes after. All of them full of love and devotion, but hiding it deep inside."

I had to laugh at the idea of my haughty grandmother ever loving anyone. "But she did," Mother insisted. "Cared for your grandfather so intensely, it was almost a joke—nearly went out of her mind when they were in Paris once, and she discovered he was infatuated with some dancer the King of Belgium was keeping."

My father turned to her in astonishment. "Who told you a wild thing like that?"

"Effie," she said. "Even after they got back to St. Paul, your father was still writing letters to this woman. So d'you know how your mother won him back? She spent a fortune on satins and plumes, and dressed up for him in private."

She raised her voice above my father's continuing disbelief. "Had little suppers served in their bedroom at midnight," she said, "With her eyes and lips painted, and let him pretend she was Cleo de Merode."

Dress-up seems to have run in the family.

## - 4 -

## MINOTAUR

The waiter who brought in the tea tray always gave me a smoldering sidelong look. His name was Ramon, but my formidable grandmother and the other ladies at the Hollywood Hotel called him Raymond. Most of the waiters there were cheerful little Filipinos, but Raymond was proudly, even arrogantly, Spanish.

He stood so straight that his back arched, and when he moved, it was with the contemptuous grace of a bullfighter. He wore a starched white jacket next to his skin, the top button coinciding with a tuft of black hair, and his trousers fit so tightly that surely he used some sort of shoehorn to get them on. He seldom spoke and never smiled—only nodded slightly when my grandmother tipped him, and departed with a glance at me so secret and portentous, it was almost a warning.

"At least Felipe always said thank you," my grandmother observed, as the door closed.

"Who's Felipe?"

"The room-service waiter, last winter," she said. "He was such a nice boy. Went to night school, and sent his mother five dollars a week."

"Isn't Raymond nice too?"

Her shrug was barely perceptible. "Raymond isn't interested in service, he's out here to get in the movies. Except he'll never make the grade."

"How come? He's real good-looking."

"Ah, but that accent!"

"Too Spanish?"

"Too Brooklyn," she said.

I had only heard a Brooklyn accent once, and that was the previous year when I was fourteen, and had been taken with some classmates on a supervised junket to Boulder Dam. All day we took notes and memorized facts, but our real education came after dark, when we boys dodged the proctor and sneaked into roaring Boulder City. Cigars gave us a look of maturity as we strolled through the huge red light district, watching the lines of hookers trying to enflame the passing johns. The girls' price was two dollars, but we were able to listen in on their sales pitches for nothing. The one from Brooklyn had a long ruffled dress and hair that seemed to have burst from a hay rack. "He ast me would I do it for a qwatah" she was indignantly telling a co-worker. "I says, 'Hell, no, I don't do it for no *qwatah.*'"

Impressed, I murmured her words over and over to myself, as if they were some maxim I could live by. Even now, a year later, there was something oddly erotic to me about the speech of Brooklyn, and I kept waiting to hear it from Raymond's lips.

I began to drop in more often on my grandmother. For years, she and my grandfather had wintered in the old Hollywood Hotel, whose squat towers and rambling gardens occupied a full city block on the shiny art-deco boulevard.

It was a comfortable time-warp for her now that she was widowed, and the whole family was careful to see she was never lonely. Not only did my sisters and I come over on Sundays, but, ever since my initial exposure to Raymond, I began dropping by on weekdays alone. These visits had to be carefully timed, since I was at school until three, and it took an hour more to get to Hollywood by bus. If I arrived later than four, tea was likely to be done with, and a glimpse of the smoldering Latin waiter lost. Even more frustrating was getting there on time, only to find Grandma having tea on the veranda, where it would be served by Carlos, an old Filipino who giggled. It forced me into thinking ahead for the first time in my life. I began telephoning her from school, saying I was on my way, and suggesting that we meet in her suite.

She had become more openly affectionate these past two years, my grandfather's death having finally widened the focus of her attention. Her voice often softened when she heard mine, and she called me "Buddy," a nickname she had always resisted. Even so, she was not to be swayed by some idle whim. "May I inquire why you find indoors so preferable to the veranda?" she asked.

I blamed it on poor Miss Brie, an old lady who often sat rocking with her on the porch. Actually, I had nothing against Miss Brie, although her hair reminded me of those gray pads that are taken out of carpet sweepers. However, she talked a lot, and I claimed she never let me get a word in. While my grandmother met this explanation with quiet irony, she put up no further resistance to our meeting in her suite. As soon as I arrived, she would phone room-service, and shortly, a tap on the door would announce Raymond, balancing the heavy tea tray high on one hand, darkly impassive except for the half-hidden glitter of his eyes. My physical response to this glance was irrepressible. The novelist I read so ravenously back then, Thomas Wolfe, called it "a stirring in the loins." There was no way to hide this phenomenon but to jam my hands in my pockets—perhaps not the easiest way to drink tea.

But then, nothing about those afternoons was entirely easy. I had hopes of converting Raymond's silent communication into comfortable small talk, so that eventually he would invite me to a movie or something. To get him started, I asked him what time it was, hoping he would tell me qwatah past four; but he just showed me his wristwatch, and let me draw my own conclusion. Another time, I called him Carlos to force him to correct me. His eyes flashed, but he did not otherwise put me right. Somebody told me that a little honest flattery made a friendship flourish, so I tried that too. "I heard Miss Brie say something very nice about you," I told him. He paused in passing the plate of cookies and waited for me to continue. "Don't you want to know what she said?" I baited.

He looked to my grandmother, and she spoke for him. "Of course he wants to know," she said, "although I've never heard Esther Brie say anything nice about anyone."

I quickly made up some compliment about his good posture. I knew it pleased him by the way he stood up even straighter, looking more than ever like a bullfighter; but he did not smile or say thank you. Instead, he made a slight formal bow, and not to me either, but to Grandma Gregg. Only when he finally carried the tea tray out into the hall again, did he flash me a look from under his half-lowered lids, re-establishing contact.

But was it contact? Suppose it was just my wishful thinking? For all I knew, these seeming signals were just an unconscious mannerism, even a tic, like that joke about the preacher who kept winking at the bride. I had to admit that, except for those searing glances, Raymond had ignored me completely. But maybe, I thought, he was just waiting for me to make the next move. However, I had already exhausted all the next-moves I could think of. Although I had worked hard at getting some genuine bed experience, I still didn't have much to draw upon. My only conquests had been boys my own age, and even these had been engineered mainly by dares and feigned sleep. Older men—Raymond was at least twenty-five—were in another league entirely, one I knew nothing about.

It was November before my efforts to be seduced made any headway. Tea was over; my grandmother slipped a tip into Raymond's hand, clicked shut her purse, and carried it back to her bedroom. Raymond flicked the usual look at me, and, hoisting the tea tray high on one hand, started to leave. Disappointed that he should take so little advantage of our first moment alone, I crossed the room and held the door to the corridor open for him. What happened next, I still have trouble explaining. Maybe while he was eyeing me, he miscalculated his distance. Or as he passed, I may have edged closer so he'd have to *squeeze* by me. At all events, we got wedged together in the doorway, and his high-held tray started to topple. I reached my free arm up to steady it. "*Don't move!*" I cried.

For an instant, we stood locked together, arms held high, every muscle tensed against a possible cascade of hot tea. He was so close, I could smell the vanilla scent of his hair oil; could feel the imprint of his whole body, belt buckle, macho bulge, and all. Already, he was trying to lower the tray, but I was still straining to hold it up high on my side. This caused the teapot to skitter down the incline. Frantically striving to level things, he thrust his side higher, just as I let mine down, precipitating a reverse rush, and I nearly missed the first words he ever spoke to me: "*Leggo da fuckin' tray!*"

His mouth had mashed against my ear, so I had only to move my head a fraction to meet his lips. And I might have done so too, except that the creamer went hurtling off the tray, and crashed to the floor.

"What's that?" my grandmother called from the bedroom. I felt a shock jolt through Raymond. Suddenly wrenching the tray free, scattering spoons and napkins, he made off down the corridor. With a frantic effort to look placid, I turned around as my grandmother swept back into the front room.

She glanced at the shattered pitcher. "How did that happen?"

"I don't know," I cried.

Her eyes searched me, and I wondered uneasily if she suspected anything. With her plumb-line posture and proud, impassive face, it was hard to tell what she was thinking. I tried reassuring myself that grandmothers probably didn't even know about such matters. Yet all too clearly, I could recall overhearing the veranda ladies discussing the King of England's liaison with Mrs. Simpson. "It all sounds made-up to me," Miss Brie had argued. "Everyone knows the King is *that-way* with men." The other ladies consulted each other over their spectacles. "What does '*that-way* with men' mean?" one of them asked. My grandmother had not looked up from her embroidery. "Nothing that will change your life, or mine," she said, crisply ending the discussion.

So even if she chose not to discuss it with anyone, she was clearly aware of the variations existing outside her sequestered world. I kept turning this fact over in my mind as I headed home that day, and realized that if she *was* wondering what was going on between Raymond and me, I had better arrange for some kind of cloud-cover.

Consequently, when I came to see her next, I brought along a girl from my drama class at school. Rosalie was rather full-blown—-could have easily passed for twenty, and had carefully cultivated a look that wasn't quite virginal. For reasons never explained, she wore a riding habit to the hotel, and used an English accent. My grandmother was gracious to her, but clearly thought she was too mature for me. Every time she called me "Buddy," I felt it was with the intention of making Rosalie feel positively venerable by contrast. I enjoyed myself enormously, however, especially in anticipating Raymond's arrival. I wanted him to see there was nothing to worry about; that he was in the hands of a master of tact and discretion. But when the tea was brought in that afternoon, the tray was carried by giggly old Carlos.

And, in fact, with Rosalie or without, every time I went to see my grandmother after that, tea was always brought in by Carlos. I wondered if Grandma had seen the wisdom of separating me and Raymond. If so, it did no good, he was on my mind all the time now. Hours that should have been devoted to homework were given over to daydreams—*piction*, I called it, a word of my own invention, half picture, half fiction. Sometimes, this was about Raymond's quick rise to movie stardom, but mostly it was about us being together in Spain. I saw myself helping him to wind into his pink sash before he went into the bull ring. When he acknowledged the cheers of the crowd, his eyes searched the stands to find me. I sailed my hat into the arena. It landed at his feet. Somehow he knew it was mine.

I fed these images by re-reading Ernest Hemingway's book about matadors, and got to be quite an authority on waving red capes to make the bull charge. These are called passes, the slow ones being veronicas, and the kind that stops a bull brusquely, recortes. I practiced both with a bath towel after my shower, and the approving smile I saw in the steamed-up mirror was Raymond's.

Sun struck with the thought of him, I cut school that Friday morning, and went to the hotel, determined not to give up until we stood reunited. Sneaking in the side door in case my grandmother was sitting on the veranda, I searched the entire first floor, then the second. I didn't bother with the elevators or main staircase since the staff wasn't allowed to use them anyway, but tiptoed up and down the uncarpeted back stairs. Time raced along on my expectancy, but it was an hour before I saw him hurrying down a dim corridor, carrying a pressed suit on a hanger. I suddenly had no breath to call out to him; only enough to follow.

Not until after he had delivered the suit did he realize I was there. For a moment, we just stared at each other. Then, with one of those hot, penetrating looks, he continued quickly down the long passage. Once again, I followed. He did not look back, but paused for an instant every time the hall turned, so I could see which direction he took. It was like the Minotaur's maze in the Greek myth I'd been taught at school, and I was completely lost by the time he stopped. Unlocking a door, he went inside without knocking. A bedroom, I wondered? An empty bedroom? Heart pounding, I edged closer—touched the brass doorknob, and then with decision, turned it.

The door opened on a steep flight of stairs, and the air that hit me was stifling. I took a quick breath, and started climbing. The tower room I came up into seemed to be the hotel's attic. Raymond was examining some piles of dusty furniture, as if they were what he had come here to check on. The stairs creaking beneath my feet surely must have warned him I had followed, and yet he suddenly faced me as if in surprise. "What'cha doin' up here?"

My stutter did not really explain. He frowned and came closer. There was no welcome in his voice. "So how come you follow me up here?"

I could only stare at him. This was not the reunion I had been dreaming of. "Lookin' for something"?" he persisted.

"No," I said, almost inaudibly.

"Yeh, yeh, yeh," he jeered. "All winter long, givin' me looks. What'cha want from me?" My mouth went completely dry. "*Huh?*" he demanded. "What the fuck do you want?" Suddenly, he thrust his hips forward, and squeezed the front of his trousers. "This?"

Somehow, I managed a heroic gesture. "*This!*" I said, and put my hand over his heart.

Or maybe I meant to do that, but never got around to it, because his next remark took my breath away. "So how much 'll you pay me?" he asked.

When I could speak, I said, "Money?"

"Sure, money," he said. "Nobody gets nothin' for nothin'. "

Even if I had been willing to pay, all I had on me was the kind of small change that seemed to infuriate people in the sex business. "I don't have any money," I said.

"But you can get some," he said. "Da old lady gives you money, I seen her."

"Just bus fare.

"So tell her you're takin' a taxi."

I was already backing away, but he moved right along with me. "Okay?" he demanded.

I shook my head. "I don't want to."

"Well, you better want to," he warned. "I wouldn't like to tell your gramma you was tryin' to get in my pants."

The menace in his voice was a revelation. I suddenly recognized that I had blundered into reality, a tough, unforgiving arena which my highly-colored daydreams had not prepared me for. Now there was not even time to picture my grandmother's horror; it was a moment for action, and I took it.

I ran so blindly, I have no memory of clattering down the stairs, or leaving the hotel; not even of crossing the Boulevard. I was only aware, at last, of squeezing into a crowded bus with an ache in my stomach and my ears hot with humiliation. This gradually changed to indignation, and then, bit by bit, I began to rescue my self-respect. In my mind, I saw myself again facing Raymond in the hotel attic; once more, heard the menace in his voice as he threatened to tell my grandmother. But this time, if only in my "piction", my eyes remained cool, and my voice level.

"She wouldn't believe you," I imagined myself saying. "But she'd believe *me!* And I'd tell her you lured me up here, and tried to molest me."

It was like waving a red rag at him. "Bullshit," he said hotly. "*Bullshit*!"

"The cops'll believe me too," I continued, my fantasy providing me with logic which had never been manifest before. "They'd know it wasn't my fault. Whoever heard of a kid molesting a grown man? I'd tell 'em you tried to force me to do it, and I'm underage. They'll throw you in jail forever, you'll be an old man when you get out!"

That stopped him in his tracks. Stopped him *brusquely*. He stood there confused and uncertain, blinking at me, and breathing with his mouth open, looking just like the bull at the moment of truth. Shifting uneasily from foot to foot, he wiped his palms down the sides of his trousers. Abruptly, he jerked his thumb toward the stairs. "Get out," he said huskily. "Get your ass outa here!"

But I was not ready to leave yet. Wanting him to appreciate that I could fight even closer to the horn—could dare any insolence now without fear of reprisal—I casually reached down and made a pass at him that was no veronica. "*Ole!*" I cried, and without looking back, jauntily sauntered downstairs.

By the time the bus reached my stop, my stomachache had miraculously vanished.

## - 5 -

## LITTLE BOY BLEW

Our eyes only met for an instant, but the voltage went right through me. Quickly, he glanced away. I held my breath, waiting for him to look around again, but he went on shoving books back onto the shelves. As he moved noiselessly about the library, I realized he wasn't actually blond. His hair was a kind of toast color, but the overhead lights transformed it into a blaze. I gave him green eyes in my imagination, but as he passed, he raised them to me again, and they were gray. His voice was so quiet, I could scarcely hear it: "Are you finding what you want?"

Actually, I had only come to the library to return some overdue books, but now, with a rush of blood to my ears, I claimed to be searching for some novel I'd heard my English teacher rave about—*Now in November*, it was called. He nodded with approval, and told me it had won the Pulitzer Prize. Hushed voices were regulation in public libraries, but somehow his whisper made everything seem so romantically clandestine that the blood left my ears and conspicuously concentrated elsewhere.

I pretended to peer at the books on the shelf behind his head, as an excuse to keep looking at him. He was handsome, perhaps even beautiful, his features sensitive, his gray eyes lustrous, large. He was shorter than I, but older by several years. There was a razor nick on his chin, the sort of detail I probably noticed because I myself didn't have to shave every day yet.

If he knew what I was up to, he gave no sign. "Over here," he directed, and led me to another aisle. Tracing his finger along the line of books, he peered at the white numbers inked on their spines. "*Now in November* must be out," he whispered. "Try again next week."

I thanked him, but added that by next week I would be gone. He looked at me in surprise. "Gone?"

I explained about my parents letting me stay in Los Angeles while they were away, so I could finish the winter term at high school. "But now that I have, I've got to go join them."

"Very far away?"

"Florida." I made a face, not at my destination, but at having to give up my independence after two sublime months on my own.

He wished me a good trip, and went back to his work. Disappointed that our conversation had led to so little, I moved along. Yet when I glanced back, he was still watching. I paused to tie my shoe. I tied it four times before he came over. "It occurs to me," he whispered, "I have a copy of *Now in November* at home. I could lend it to you, if you should happen to be around here tomorrow."

I was not only at the library the following day, but an hour earlier, and with my hair cut. I scarcely got to talk to him, however. Too many people were around. He acted as if he didn't know me, and just pointed to the front desk. "I left the book for you there."

I tried to read it on the bus, going back to the house where I was rooming, but neither then nor after dinner could I seem to concentrate. Seeing him even briefly had set off that agitation that had been plaguing me lately. My heart would start pounding in the tips of my fingers, there was a constant strain on my fly, and the languor in me had nothing to do with drowsiness. All the contraries in the world seemed to be dividing me up, so that half of me would be in a tantrum, while the other half was already saying I'm sorry. My father called these tempests of mine by the newspaper nickname for the turbulent Santa Anna wind that periodically swept over the city: *Little Boy Blew.* It made a childish spectacle of itself, whipping trees, stirring up dust devils, sending dogs scurrying under beds. "Hey, there," Dad would cry, turning up his collar when I'd start rampaging, "the *Little Boy* is back!"

For all my turmoil, I managed to get through the book by two in the morning. The part I liked best was the fly leaf, where I discovered he had written *Property of Robert Standish.* It was the perfect name for him, I thought—calm, strong, aristocratic. I liked it better than the two staccato sounds of my own name which had the same beat as fuck you.

To put myself in Robert's class, I shaved before I went to the library that afternoon. He was at the front desk this time. When I handed his book back to him, he whispered, "When do you leave?"

"Tomorrow at noon."

He turned this over in his mind. "I wish there were time for us to have dinner together, but—" He sighed.

I let my disappointment show. "It's all right," I said pathetically.

Suddenly he came to a decision. "How do you feel about Chinese food?"

I had no fixed response to it, but had he asked my opinion of mud pies, my burst of enthusiasm would have been the same.

He drove by for me at six-thirty that night. I had unpacked my suitcases to get at my best clothes, but next to Robert, trim in his tan corduroy suit, I felt tacky, all elbows and Adam's apple. He wasn't a lot more talkative behind the wheel of his car than he had been in the stacks, but when we got to the chop suey place, far downtown, he began to open up—did all the ordering, showed me how to use chopsticks, filled me in on the graduate work he was doing at USC. He did not laugh a lot, or joke at all, but when the fortune in his rice cookie promised him good news, he smiled at me as if I were its harbinger.

It was late by the time he got me back to my door that night. The house where I was rooming was comfortable, but rigidly genteel, and the students who lived there were not allowed visitors after nine. However, our landlady had gone to bed by now, and I did not argue with myself about asking Robert to come upstairs. He smiled when he saw my suitcases lying open on the floor, the clothes still scatt ered about. "You'll have to work fast to get them re-packed by train time," he said.

"Oh, I'm not going by train" I said, not thinking.

"How then? Bus?"

I fumbled for an answer. Times were still hard for so many people, and it was embarrassing to admit to the silver spoon. Still, I hated to lie to anyone as fine as he. "My dad thought it'd be educational," I confessed. "I'm going through the Panama Canal."

Once more I was aware of how sympathetic his eyes were. He was very understanding. Everything about him was understanding. Yet nothing was happening. Our facing each other on the faded plush sofa, with the door locked and the bed so close by, should have suggested something to him, yet he just sat there being tactful and understanding. I traced an intricate little pattern on the plush upholstery with my forefinger, and gradually transferred this to his corduroy knee. I was only inches away from target, when he seized my hand, restraining it, and blurted out what had apparently been inhibiting him. "*How old are you?*"

I lied to him after all, and said eighteen.

Not persuaded, he searched my face; but it was too late now. I thrust nearer, and suddenly his arms were around me, his open mouth upon mine.

This had never happened before. I had enjoyed a certain amount of carnal adventure since my coming-out at prep school, but no one, as yet, had kissed me. Perhaps there hadn't been time during those quick and furtive encounters. In the rush for crescendo, the grace notes had been lost, and until this minute, not even missed. Now, the surprise of Robert's tongue in my mouth set off a tempest in me—not a little-boy tempest, this time, but hot, wet, and driving. I wanted this astonishing innovation to go on for at least forever, but things went too fast, and next I knew, we were on the bed, as ravening as starved animals, as intricately locked together as a Jack of Hearts.

It was only after Robert had left that I began to get some perspective. I was still clothed, but my disarray was more specific than nakedness. My face, reflected in the mirror, was flushed, my eyes luminous, and an unfamiliar bliss told me I was hopelessly, helplessly in love. *In love,* and with only those worn-out old words to express it! Yet I could not wait to share them with Robert. My impulse was to run downstairs and phone him at once. And I would have, but it was late, and he lived with his parents. Nothing, however, *nothing* would keep me from being at the library when he got to work the next day at noon.

Noon? High as I was flying, this word suddenly reached me and brought me back to earth. Noon was when I was due to catch the boat-train to San Pedro harbor. I thought it over for about three seconds, and then returned to mid-air. The trip through the Panama Canal was an obvious impossibility now. My shirts and socks, still strewn over the floor, became a symbol of my decision to stay here with Robert. I grabbed up everything that could be folded and stuffed it back into my bureau, shoving the rest under the bed.

Of course my parents would have to be told I would not be coming to Florida. That was almost my first thought when I woke up the next morning. Naturally, I could not tell them what had changed my mind, but I would think up some good reason, and they would probably give their blessings—they were always telling me I must learn to make my own decisions.

Telephoning long-distance was still an ordeal, especially if you were calling collect. It meant having to discuss everything with the operators, and getting transferred around with lots of clicks before connection was possible. My mother answered at last, and when she had accepted the charges, I told her I wanted to stay on in Los Angeles and take some courses at USC. She was a remarkable woman, imaginative and enthusiastic, usually sympathetic to my projects. But not this time. From the dry tone of her voice, it was almost as if she had expected this call. It was the same with my father when he got on the phone. His insistence that I sail today as planned was quiet, specific, and almost eerily in advance of my arguments. "I want you to be on the boat when it docks in Miami next week," he concluded. "All right?"

I could not fight him, but I would not reassure him. "Maybe," I said, and hung up.

The consequence of this call was that, within the half-hour, my stately Grandmother Gregg drove up in a taxi. As we had already said goodbye the day before, it was clear that my parents had telephoned her right after talking to me, and urged her to make sure I took the boat-train. "I came to help you pack," she said, with suspect gaiety. There was nothing I could do to stop her. The suitcases were dragged out from under the bed, the shirts and shorts taken from the bureau.

She packed carefully, almost warily, as if looking for proof that something illicit had been going on here. I knew she couldn't have heard about Robert's visit this quickly, but I suddenly thought of Rosalie, the girl from my drama class whom I had brought over to Grandma's hotel several times as a blind. Chances were, this red herring had worked all too well, and Grandma had written my father and mother that I was in the clutches of a man-hungry older blonde. This would account for their sudden offer of the cruise through the Canal—anything to lure me back to parental supervision. It would also explain why they were so adamant when I tried to back out of the trip at the last minute.

There was no way to avoid being shipped out now, and not even time to telephone Robert and pledge unchanging love. Grandma's taxi driver helped carry out my luggage, and once we were in the cab, Grandma settled back and patted my hand. "You're going to have a wonderful voyage," she said, affably now. "I wish I were going with you."

I was almost afraid she was, and the taxi driver too. They stayed with me right up to the moment I climbed aboard the boat-train. As it finally pulled out, I saw her waving at me, her white-gloved hand isolated in the sunlight—the same sunlight that, at that very minute, was probably making golden dazzle of Robert's hair. He would be climbing the library steps now, and as he pulled open the door, I could feel him missing me already.

My fancies about him were fancy, all right, displacing the most impressive reality. I scarcely noticed the shuddering blast that announced the ship was weighing anchor; barely saw the crowded dock recede, or heard the band on board briskly playing *Siboney*. Once at sea, I ignored the shuffleboard and movies to take solitary walks along the deck, or gaze deeply into the churning wake, wondering if, at that exact moment, he was thinking about me. Moonlight provided a further dimension for reverie. Eating an orange at midnight, I arranged the pieces of peel into the shape of his initials, R. S. This may have fallen short of a sonnet, but at least was total commitment.

Although I did not seem to notice Acapulco, Panama City, or the famous locks, it was only by will power that I avoided having a good time on board the ship. A good-looking girl from Beverly Hills taught me to French inhale, and a young man from First Class often sneaked down to Cabin Class to sit in the sun with us. At night, there was dancing, and the band was great, except for that little tendency to strike up *Siboney* every time a flaming dessert was carried to a table.

I left the ship at Havana, where a smaller boat was to connect me with Miami. As there was a twenty-hour stopover, I had been booked into a little hotel. With all of Cuba's old-regime luxury and decadence waiting to be discovered, I chose to stay in my room and continue a letter to Robert, which was now a document of some twelve pages. Only hunger interrupted me. The desk clerk gave me directions to a famous restaurant, but by the time I had gone five blocks, I was lost. Fortunately, I ran into the young man from First Class, who was lost too. We strolled along, both of us talking at once, grinning when women in dark doorways surreptitiously called to us.

"Where are you staying?" I asked.

"Well, actually, nowhere," he said. "Fact is, I got put off the boat."

"But why?"

He laughed sheepishly. "I didn't have a ticket."

I wasn't sure I believed his story. Still, in case he really was marooned here, I took him to dinner, and later let him bunk in my hotel room. It was tropically hot, and we slept under a single sheet. At some undetermined hour, he put his hand lightly on my arm. I blinked open my eyes in the darkness, but did not move. He blew faintly on the back of my neck, and edging closer, asked if I felt like a little fun. Still I didn't react—just lay there, thinking fixedly of Robert, and trying to breathe regularly. Apparently it convinced him I was fast asleep, because pretty soon he yawned and gave up.

This was my first experience with being faithful, and I was so pleased with myself, I nearly turned around and hugged him.

I was afraid the Little Boy tempests would sweep back when I reached Florida, but the small college town, asleep in the middle of the state, seemed to nourish reverie. Or anyway, it did at first. I was content to lie out in the sun every day, reliving my one night with Robert, digging into every instant of it, triumphantly extracting and savoring each detail. Only when repetition had worn these images down to words did I write them in my journal. At night, I worked on my letters to him. Since I didn't know his home address, I mailed them to the library. With the same devotion, I waited by the front gate each morning to save the mailman a few final steps, in case he had a letter for me.

Sometimes he did have, but not from Robert. Gradually, I came to understand the reason why. The head librarian had probably put his mail aside for him, and then forgot to tell him. And if he wasn't getting my letters, how could he know where to send his replies? He could even be thinking I had found someone new.

To assure him I hadn't, I called him long distance. His mother kept answering the phone, however, and I kept hanging up in panic. Bit by bit, my emotions resumed such turbulence, they were nearly leveling my parents' house. "Come take a walk, Bud," my father urged, one night. We strolled down the dark road, him swinging his walking stick in great arcs. "Rosalie's not the only girl in the world, y'know," he said. "There are lots of others just as nice. Matter of fact, the college here is full of real charmers, so if you'd like to take a few courses when the spring term begins—"

I was sixteen, still young for college entry, but my father was teaching a seminar on investments there, and he used his influence to get me enrolled. Yet nothing seemed to give me any relief. I was forced to wait out every day and every night until June finally came, ending the school year and freeing my family to return to California. Invisibly pushed by me, we left for the airport an hour after my father's final lecture.

Barely pausing to dash some water in my face on our arrival in Los Angeles, I grabbed a bus for the library and Robert. Since I didn't know whether he would be on the afternoon shift or the evening, it was essential to arrive on the stroke of six so as to catch him coming or going. But traffic hardly moved. It seemed to me that night had fallen by the time I got to the familiar brick building. My heart was thundering, and I scarcely had the strength to run up the front steps.

Robert saw me almost as soon as I pushed open the door. Remembering how up-tight he got at work, I tried to hide my excitement. He hid his too, and with a barely perceptible move of the head, signaled me to follow him back into the stacks. I could scarcely keep my hands off him, but people were all around, so we pretended to be looking for a book. "When did you get back?" he whispered. Every time I tried to answer, somebody came up, demanding his assistance.

I would have been willing to sit down at the magazine table and wait for him to get off work, but he suggested it might be better for him to come pick me up after the library closed at nine. I jotted down my home address, and left it sticking out of a volume of Balzac. As I left, our eyes met, and that voltage went through me again, just like the first time I had seen him.

Dazzled, breathless, I somehow got home. My mother had left out some supper for me. Though I wasn't hungry, I ate it, lest my stomach gurgle when Robert and I were alone. I rushed through a shower, shaved of course, and put on my white suit. A moment later, I changed to blue jeans, so the family wouldn't get suspicious at such unaccustomed splendor.

Fortunately, my parents and sisters had already gone to their rooms. I sat down by a front window to wait for Robert, and almost immediately sprang up again, hearing the blare of a horn out in the street. It was not him, however. To keep from looking too eager, I opened a book and, infinitely casual, lit a cigarette. By nine-fifteen, I had smoked two to the tip. Of course, I reminded myself, I must give him time to drive here from the library. To save him a minute, I went outside and waited by the curb. Around quarter to ten, it occurred to me that I wouldn't be able to hear the telephone out there, in case he called to say he would be a little late. I hurried back into the house, and waited equidistant between phone and front door, leaning first toward one, then the other.

Not for the first time, but more strongly now, questions kept nagging me. Where was he? Why didn't he get here? Maybe the head librarian had made him stay late. Or he could have been in a traffic accident. Yet I found I wasn't believing these excuses. I was remembering instead the tension in his face when he saw me again tonight. I was recalling all those letters he had not answered. I was taking into account that the declarations of love had only come from me. I was beginning to know I had been kidding myself along.

Not that this made any immediate difference. I kept right on promising God anything, if Robert would only show up. And when this did not deliver him to my door, I clenched my eyes shut, cramped the muscles in my gut, and *willed* him to appear.

Not until midnight did I resign myself to the fact that he would not come—knew he had never even intended to. I knew something else too, something so hard to admit, it took three tries before I could find the words: the experience that had been a soul-seizing romance to me had only been a one-night stand for him.

It is tempting to say that with this admission, I grew up. Yet I'm not sure I did entirely, since that frantic tempest sometimes sweeps through me even yet. But the little boy was gone forever.

## - 6 -

## THE PARLEZ-VOUS QUESTION

She leafed through my drawings so quickly, I was afraid she didn't like them. Suddenly, she fixed her little blue eyes on me. "Know what you should do?" she demanded. "Show these to Henri de Chatillon the minute you hit Paris, he might be able to do something for you. He's terribly important in the fashion world there, knows simply everyone—Coco Chanel, Erte, Andre Gide—"

She mentioned these names as if they were famous, but I was seventeen years old, and what did I know? Still, I smiled and nodded, not wanting to spoil her fun—she adored bringing

Henri de Chatillon, by Diego

people together, pulling strings, making matches. Her name was Mary Sullivan, and she managed the book shop at the Waldorf-Astoria. I had met her there the day after my parents and I arrived in New York. While they were browsing for something to read on the voyage, I asked about a French phrase book. "Not that I really need one," I told her. "I've had two years of French at school."

"Then you'll love this book, darling," she said, and pulled a red paperback from the shelves. "It's slangy and fun, and should keep you out of trouble. Unless, of course, you're in the *mood* for trouble—" Her smile was oddly intimate. "—and aren't we all, every now and then?"

Her question dazzled me. Grown-ups didn't usually talk to me like this. I let her convince me I needed this book, just to keep her talking this way. As if we were equals. As if we were co-conspirators. As if she somehow knew my secret and even approved of it. A half-hour after I left her shop, I returned on the pretext of buying a biography of Marie Antoinette. I was there for the rest of the afternoon, and in between customers, she talked to me about proofs. Actually, it turned out, she was talking about Proust, but it made no difference as I knew nothing about the one or the other. What did matter was that she apparently believed I was an adult.

Perhaps it was my height that fooled her. I was by now over six feet tall, a condition my sister aggravated with the nickname "Stretch." Mary, herself, was short, exuberant, with the blaze of high blood pressure in her cheeks. She was a few years into her forties, an age my mother's friends back in Los Angeles were careful to camouflage; but she dressed haphazardly, with her hair heaped precariously on top of her head, rather as if she had flung it up in the air and run under it.

As her working hours seemed to be a perpetual at-home, I dropped by the book shop the next afternoon. Her other guests were young and mostly male without being primarily masculine—the Jackal Pack, as she affectionately called them. Every day, they darted in for an exchange of gossip, a word of reassur

Mary Sullivan

ance, or just to see who else was there. Each of them seemed to be her best friend, and almost immediately, I was her best friend too. On the day before my family and I sailed, she let me treat her to a sandwich at Child's Restaurant. It was then that I showed her my drawings, and there that she drafted a letter of introduction to Henri de Chatillon.

I mailed it to him the Monday I arrived in Paris, and to support her glowing opinion of my talent, enclosed one of my drawings. Yet by Wednesday, I was already hoping he wouldn't call me. Those first few days in Paris had laid bare a sobering fact: despite my two years of study, I couldn't understand French the way the French spoke it. I understood easily when Americans spoke it—even when the Dutch tourists at the hotel rattled it off—but a Parisian had only to open his mouth, and I was on a round-trip to nowhere. Maybe I was trying too hard. Maybe they were talking too fast. Either possibility warned me not to push my luck with M. de Chatillon.

All hope was lost, when on Thursday, he telephoned. I scarcely recognized my own name, the way he pronounced it. Before he could say anything more, I asked him to speak very slowly. So he spoke very slowly in perfect English. "Let me expect you at three on Saturday," he said. "Bring some more examples of your art work, and we will see what we can do about them."

Ordinarily, I dressed in a rush, but on that Saturday, I agonized over which necktie to wear, and even looked in the mirror to part my hair. "If I'm not back by dinner, don't wait," I told my parents. They wanted to know where I was going. It was the kind of thing that made me groan. I loved them, of course, but the new image of myself as an adult didn't include having a father and mother supervising every move. I made up some story about going to the Louvre with a chum from school, and when they agreed to this, I slipped away, gloriously on my own, ready to begin my career.

My *career!* That word set me on fire! Theatre was still my first choice, but art was a decent secondary vocation, should M.

de Chatillon have plans to launch me in it. This could take courage on his part, because not everyone was going to understand my drawings. They were the next thing to handwriting, a style I had invented in class to keep the teachers from realizing I wasn't taking notes on *Silas Marner* or the War of 1812. The trick was never to lift the pen from the paper—even the intricate parts like ears and toes could be accommodated by that one continuous black line. My sister Sharlie said my pictures looked like a couple of wire coat hangers mating. But Sharlie would not be so flip when I became the first American teenager to have a one-man show in Paris.

M. de Chatillon himself opened the door. "Welcome, dear boy," he cried. And then, with a glance that swept from my shoes to my cowlick: "*Mon Dieu,* you *are* tall!" He walked around me, straightened the handkerchief in my breast pocket, then casually stretched up and kissed me on the mouth; casually reached down and groped me. My heart sank. I was not inexperienced, but he seemed very old, forty-five or something. However, he was merely being prudent, he explained. "—necessary to assure myself that you understood the idiom, as it were. A mistake higher up could be grotesque."

"Higher up?"

"Very high up," he said. "The pinnacle!"

I didn't understand what he meant—possibly another allusion to my height. As it was, I had to hunch down, so as not to tower over him. Yet what M. de Chatillon lacked in stature, he made up for in taste. Everything in his apartment was spectacular. His portraits of himself by famous artists. His Louis XlV furniture. His boyfriend.

Especially his boyfriend. Sebastian was probably twenty-two, suntanned and handsome, with eyebrows like dark comets. The thing I liked best about him was his conversation—he chattered along in French, and I could make out every word he said. It was the first time, I admitted, that I had been able to understand French as the French themselves speak it.

"But he is South American," M. de Chatillon told me. "He

speaks French no better than you do."

He tousled my hair slightly to make me appear younger, and persuaded me to get rid of my necktie so as to look more American. At last, he hustled us down the great staircase, and out to his smart little roadster. I was to sit up in front with him, he said, and Sebastian could ride in the rumble seat. The dark comets instantly collided. Sebastian announced he would never sit in the rumble seat. *Never!* Mr. de Chatillon's eyes widened dangerously, and he hissed something I did not understand. The South American climbed into the little back seat, but managed to give its leather upholstery a good kick. M. de Chatillon's nostrils pinched. "*Berthe aux Grands Pieds!*" His words sounded like pistol shots.

"Beg pardon?" I said.

He translated impatiently. "Big-Feets Bertha. A creature of great clumsiness from the last century—but it ruins it to explain."

He was calmer when we arrived at an ornate apartment house. An open elevator hoisted us up an iron-lace shaft, down which I would have gladly sunk again as the hum of relentless French on the top floor drew closer. Actually, there were only about a dozen guests in the rooms we entered, but all were people of opinion, and so sounded like more. Sebastian immediately left us for a group of young men, and someone with a beard sidetracked M. de Chatillon into a controversy. I couldn't understand a word of it, of course, and waited with perspiration running down my face. The apartment was jungle hot, with tropical plants crowding every table and shelf—ferns, giant philodendrons, even a young coconut tree that brushed the ceiling, reminding me to hunch. New people continued to arrive. I kept wagging the cardboard tube I carried, in hope that someone would ask what it was, and either give me an excuse to unroll my drawings, or make M. de Chatillon remember why we were here. When I finally caught his eye, he patted my cheek. "Have no fear," he said. "He is expected any minute."

"He?"

"Yes," he said, and abandoned the subject, as if once again asked to explain *Berthe aux Grands Pieds.*

I found Sebastian, and asked what M. de Chatillon had up his sleeve. Perhaps the phrase is not a familiar one in French, or anyway, in Sebastian's French, for he examined it dubiously, shrugged, and allowed that it could possibly be Jean.

"Jean?" I asked. "An art critic, or something?"

"No, no, no, *stupide*! Jean Cocteau. An artist. A poet, a novelist, a film-maker. The *pinnacle!*" He postured contemptuously, and droned out some non-sequiturs which he claimed was the narrative from *The Blood of a Poet*. "Oh, it is to laugh, so pretentious!" he added, moving along.

"And they're old friends?" I persisted, following after him. "This Jean and M. de Chatillon?"

"Friends?" He looked back at me, and shrugged. "Sometimes at four o'clock, maybe. But not at three or five."

It was, in fact, around five o'clock that a little silence raced through the room, and the guests glanced toward the foyer expectantly. Several of the young men scurried in that direction. "Come!" said Henri de Chatillon, at last.

Grasping me by the cardboard tube, he marched across the room to where the young men were already transfixed by a sonorous speaking voice. It belonged to a man whose youth seemed to dry up as we drew nearer. He was not tall, although his gauntness and high drift of dark hair helped create that illusion. His face was narrow, sharp, and as he spoke, his quick, almost feverishly brilliant eyes swept from face to face. M. de Chatillon greeted him with a knowing little smile, and pushed me forward showily, as if I, rather than my drawings, had been brought here for inspection. The speaker momentarily included me in his gaze, but apparently found nothing remarkable, because he went right on talking. I suddenly had the feeling that M. de Chatillon had intended me as a gift, and that it had just been rejected.

Annoyed by this unresponsiveness, M. de Chatillon nudged me nearer, and as his friend did not wind up his discourse, suddenly cut in. "Jean—" It would have been easier to divert the Seine with a mustard paddle. Jean swept right on. M. de Chatillon shushed several of the young men who were shushing him, and again tried to interrupt. It seemed only to make Jean more eloquent.

Impatiently, M. de Chatillon tugged the cardboard tube from my hand and thrust it out to him. Jean, droning now in that distinctive way that Sebastian had parodied, absently closed his fingers around the cylinder, but did not look at it; merely used it to emphasize his points. Not until the suspense was in danger of suffocating me did he shake the drawings out of the tube. People crowded closer as he began to study my work. Gradually his flow of words slowed, and by reverse ratio, he leafed through the pages faster and faster. Abruptly, and with two sketches yet to be seen, he bundled them all back into M. de Chatillon's hands, and without explanation, resumed his discourse.

M. de Chatillon stiffened and once more interrupted, apparently demanding to know what was wrong with the drawings. Jean answered loftily, and I tugged M. de Chatillon's arm, needing him to translate. The way he looked at me now, I couldn't tell whose side he was on. "M. Cocteau claims your drawings counterfeit his style."

I blinked. "What?"

"He says that everyone *knows* how he draws, and you have simply copied it."

I was so astonished by the accusation that I should have been speechless, and yet there I was, wide-eyed and big-mouthed, blurting my innocence to Jean Cocteau in second-year French. I couldn't possibly have copied his work, I assured him—I had never seen any of it, never heard of it, hadn't even known who he was until just a moment ago.

I probably said more before the look on his face and the reaction of his coterie warned me I had made a blunder. Just in case anyone had missed it, however, M. de Chatillon snatched up my remark and echoed it the length of the room. *What?* he crowed, with malicious delight. *Was it possible? Someone who had never heard of Jean Cocteau?* Each time he repeated this, he made it sound more like a repudiation of the Cross.

I tried to explain myself more clearly, but M. de Chatillon instantly processed this into a weapon too. Cocteau cut back with a scorn so precisely crafted, it could have passed for a blade. Other guests began hurrying over to hear, standing on tiptoe, watching the barbs fly back and forth as if at a tennis match, sometimes sneaking a glance at me.

I knew no way to die unobtrusively. I longed to run out of the apartment, but M. de Chatillon was still clutching my drawings, and I couldn't leave without them. Standing there, terminally tall and utterly on my own, I became aware that one bystander was watching my misery steadfastly, and in sudden indignation I turned to stare her down.

She met my eyes without embarrassment. Observing me for an instant more, she plucked a grape from a bowl of fruit, weighed it thoughtfully in her hand, then tossed it to me. I shouldn't have even lifted my hand to catch it, but I did; shouldn't have eaten it either, but I did that too, and then twiddled the seeds between my fingertips, wondering why I hadn't just swallowed them. She flicked her thumb carelessly at an open window. I repeated her gesture, and the seeds sailed out. She smiled, showing a smudge of lipstick on her teeth. Warily, I pretended interest in a large cactus beside her as an excuse to come closer. Without surprise, she took my arm and comfortably strolled me away from the recriminations, silently pointing out the bizarre hybrids of familiar plants.

She was, herself, an odd combination of exotic and household. Her feet were sturdy, but bare in flat sandals, and though her body had begun to thicken, the portrait of a young girl was painted over her face. Her eyes looked out of black encirclement, and a shaved pencil point had been twirled high on her cheekbone, leaving a neat, almost imperceptible dot. It suggested that flirtation was an old habit, and yet there was nothing coquettish in her manner: her glance was direct, her mouth ironic.

Since she was wearing a hat, it didn't seem likely she was my hostess, and yet she had a proprietary way about everything in the apartment, smoothing dust from the plants with her thumb, testing the soil for moisture. Pausing significantly by the shaggy, almost simian trunk of a tree fern, she crouched slightly, and with an ape-like grimace, strummed her ribs.

Even as I laughed, I thought of my father, who depended almost exclusively on pantomime to communicate with the French. It made me wonder if my new friend also had a language problem, and tactfully, I asked her the *parlez-vous* question. She replied in voluble French, but with a foreign accent so robust that even I could discern it. The moment I realized she was in the same boat as myself, I lost my fear, and found I could understand her, the same as I had the Dutch tourists or Sebastian. We were like the lame among the lame, suddenly finding a freedom to dance.

She knew the wisdom of keeping a man busy with questions. What did one call such shoes as I wore? (Saddle.) Did Americans think there would be a war? (No.) How old was I? (Twenty, I said, but she smiled knowingly.) Her French faltered occasionally while she searched for a word, but if I did the same, she brusquely prompted me to *parle* up, drum-rolling her R's.

From time to time, I glimpsed M. de Chatillon and Sebastian in the crowd, but not until my new friend had gone did I rejoin them. M. de Chatillon tossed my drawings to me, and led me to the elevator. As we returned to the ground floor, he made no effort to hide his mortification at having sponsored me. His eyes were cold, his voice crisp, his words so swift and incessant that I had to remind him again that I could not understand Frenchmen's French. "What nonsense!" he countered, irritably and in English. "You and Madame were jabbering away, and you understood her clearly enough."

I tried to explain that it was because we were both foreigners and our bad accents compatible, but this only aggravated him more. "The accent of Burgundy is not foreign," he cried.

"There is nothing foreign about her, in all this country she writes the French most pure." He reeled off the names of her novels, measured the height of her fame, and added, as if in defense of the tricoleur, "Do not dare to mock our great Colette!"

Her name was not known to me at the time, but I gathered from M. de Chatillon's outrage that I had earned a permanent place beside Big-Feets Bertha. Very little more was said as they drove me back to my hotel. Not much to my surprise, I rode in the rumble seat.

## - 7 –

## FULL-TIME HOPSCOTCH

It was dark on the beach except for the bonfire, but I could see the scar on his face as he came rushing up. It was by his right sideburn, white against his suntan, and even in that split second, made me think of a young swordsman in some romantic novel. Then I hit the sand. Touch football is what we were supposed to be playing, but for some reason, he had tackled me. "No, dammit, *touch!*" a bossy blonde dyke yelled at him. "You're only allowed to *touch*!" So that's what he did the next time he tackled me—slid his hand over my fly and touched me. I began to like the game rather better.

When I could do so inconspicuously, I asked the blonde who he was. "Oh, that's Briney," she said. "Brian Barlow. Works at the Laguna Hotel, you must've seen him on the beach there."

"Lifeguard?"

"Probably that too," she said. "He's everything else—bellboy, elevator operator, bottle-washer. Summer job stuff."

The picnic broke up around eleven. As I started walking back to the beach house where I was visiting relatives, an old Chevy pulled up, and Briney looked out. He was driving one of the girls home, and offered to give me a lift too. Actually, my destination was nearer than hers, but he took *her* home first, then headed back through the center of town. "Turn here," I told him; but he didn't. "Where are we going?" I asked.

"My place," he said. "Okay?"

I shrugged. Not that I was indifferent—quite the opposite—but I kept feeling out of my league with him. I had never had any luck with guys this good- looking. Even his flaws were attractive. Crew cuts were so obligatory that summer that curly hair looked freakish. But not on him. The old sweatshirt he wore was shapeless, and his trousers were baggy. What redeemed them was the way his lithe body thrust against the loose folds in graphic outline. And then there was that scar! It looked like an H.- H for Handsome. H for Heartbreaker. H for Humpy.

"Go to college?" he was asking me. I smiled glassily and nodded. "Sophomore," he guessed. But I couldn't even claim that. I was still just a freshman, having only entered Rollins after spring break. "I went to UCLA," he said. "Oh, just for a year—-had to drop out and earn a living. But I'll be going back for my degree any time now."

He talked so much about returning to school, I suddenly wondered if he was afraid I thought he was just a bellboy. It hadn't occurred to me until now that, for all his conspicuous assets, he might be feeling inadequate too. The possibility seemed to ease my resistance to him. Gradually, I began to settle back and relax, even to kid with him.

We turned down a dirt road and drove through a field, finally pulling up by a little plywood house. I followed him inside. The room was dark, smelling of kerosene and oilcloth. When he lit the oil lamp, a hundred moths outside began to tap against the window screens. He held up a bottle of scotch. "No, thanks," I said.

"Rather have something soft?"

It got me laughing: in this increasingly intimate circumstance, what would I do with anything soft? He laughed too, and we began to get rid of our clothes.

Even when he blew out the lamp, I continued to see his body in the dark—the broad shoulders, the suntan that made his white flanks look even more naked. He was better-looking than me, I reflected, but I was better hung, and this gave me a moment of self-confidence. Then the excitement swallowed up everything.

When I awoke the next morning, I was alone in bed with sun in my eyes. Eggs were sizzling in a frying pan, and Briney was calling from the kitchen, "Get up, I've got to be at work in ten minutes."

He drove me back to my relatives' house, getting me there before my overnight absence had been noticed. We did not mention meeting again when we said goodbye, but later, on the bus trip back to Los Angeles, I began wishing I had given him my address in case he ever came into town. The restlessness I felt persisted when I got home. An odd loneliness followed me up to my room. One-night stands were not supposed to feel like this. I went to bed early, only to be awakened by my sister calling up the stairs: someone named Briney was on the phone. Somehow I kept my voice level when I picked up the receiver. "How'd you get my number?" I asked.

"I went back to see your relatives," he said. We talked for twenty minutes. We talked even longer the next night, and on the third afternoon, I took the bus back to Laguna. I told my parents I was going to stay with friends for a few days, but secrectly, I was thinking in terms of forever. Our first week together tested that idea rigorously. For one thing, I had very little money. For another, he was at the hotel all day. This was no summer job as I had been told, but his year-round work. While he was on duty bell-hopping, I killed time at the beach, waiting for him to be free. He was popular with the summer crowd, and introduced me to everyone he knew, mostly college students. Yet this scene wasn't for me. The only alternative to volleyball was cruising, and I was afraid of losing the focus of my feeling for him. I began to spend more time at the summer shack, exploring and glorying in this broad back-acreage. The far end tipped up into a hill, from which I could see miles of tall grass, burned blond and hazardous by the July sun. There was little breeze, and no sound except for the singing of insects, one note sustained so insistently, it passed for silence. I hiked about in hacked-off dungarees and some Mexican sandals that stank when they got wet. In a few days, I was so brown, Briney claimed I looked like a knotted leather thong.

There was nothing to do there, yet no day was long enough. The plywood house needed paint and got it. I planted tomato seedlings and dug irrigation trenches. At six, I walked through the field, and was waiting by the mailbox when Briney turned off the highway. Our conversation instantly picked up where it had left off that morning, and rushed through the long twilight, changing into another kind of communication after the lamp was blown out. Mosquitoes whined in the darkness, forcing us to smear our bodies with citronella. I hated the smell of it then, but now if I catch a whiff, it flashes a ghost-happiness through me that is almost like pain.

On weekend nights, we played. Briney loved good times, and had a child's gift of creating them out of nothing. "There'll be three of us," he told Mona, the head waitress at a local restaurant, one night. "We're having Katherine Hepburn to dinner." Mona, part of the secret life in Laguna, knew his ways, and smiled as she led us to a table in the patio. He took out a two-color picture of the actress, which he had torn from the Sunday paper, and pinned it to a chair. "She'll have a martini, and so will my friend," he told Mona. "Just an olive for me." He carried the whole thing off with great charm, including Hepburn in every discussion, and easing away from questions she might not choose to answer. Although he was twenty-four, this kind of make-believe still played a great part in his life. Yet some core of practicality that was almost a warning seemed to tell him that games and daydreams would never give him the kind of future he wanted. At night, we would sit at the kitchen table until bedtime, discussing his return to school. What did I think of Berkeley, he wanted to know? Had I ever heard of Antioch? How much was the tuition at Rollins? Why had I decided to study there?

I explained that it was because of my father. Every fall, he interrupted his work, and went to this little Southern campus to teach a seminar on practical business experience. Briney took in every word of this: his mother's early divorce had left him with a continuing curiosity about fathers. What was my dad's first name, he wanted to know? What did he look like? Had he found out about me? Everything I told him set off a comparison with a college professor he knew, who came to the hotel every August. "It's him who keeps pushing me," he explained.

"Pushing you?"

"To go back to college. He thinks I could make something of my life. Y'know—something *fine*!"

Abruptly, he scrambled over to the bureau, and pulled a pack of letters from under his tumble of socks and shorts. "He taught at Oberlin till he retired," he told me reverently. "History. He says the past is the greatest teacher in the world."

His name was Daniel C. Ellison, but Briney always called him "the Prof." The excerpts he read from his letters had a fatherly ring, even when they got a bit testy about Briney's happy-go-lucky life-style—"full-time hopscotch," the Prof called it. "Don't put off your education any further, Brian, damn it," he wrote. "Youth isn't forever. Suddenly you'll be forty, and still trying to live off your tips." Briney and I smiled at each other. We knew what he said was true. We just didn't believe it.

Even now, Briney was getting ready for him and his wife to arrive at the hotel; he read ten pages of Douglas Southall Freeman every day; neatened up his white service jackets, saw to it that the Ellisons would get a room that faced the ocean. I asked him how the Prof could swing such expense on a teacher's pension. Briney shrugged. "Probably has money of his own."

"Then why not ask him to help you out with some tuition?"

Briney drew himself up loftily. "I'd never ask him for

money."

"But if he secretly saw to it that the tuition was paid?"

He laughed. "You sound just like my mother!"

"How come?"

"Oh, y'know—-she's always looking for someone to stand treat." He joked about her often, but adored her. Her name was Helene, but she was called Tikki, short for Rikki Tikki Tavi. She sounded like great fun to me, sort of the madcap heiress type. There had been lots of money in the family, but it was gone now, and she had never gotten used to it. She lived on a sportsman-friend's yacht off nearby Newport Beach, but used Briney's rural mailbox as her address. This way, her creditors would be out of luck if they came here looking for her.

But nobody much came to the plywood house. That's why I thought it was Briney, home for lunch, when I heard the car door slam one noon. I was taking a shower, and hollered, "I'm in here!" A moment later, a smartly dressed woman peered into the shower stall. I turned away convulsively, trying to hide my nakedness behind my hand. "Well, hello!" she cried. "You *are* a long drink of water, aren't you!" She looked me up and down, then disappeared.

I wrapped a towel around me, and followed after her. She was good-looking in the same way Briney was, only more sleek, a brunette of a certain age, with the shoulder-length glamour-bob so popular just then with debutantes and divorcees. "You must be Briney's new boyfriend," she said.

I tensed up, afraid that this was going to be one of those confrontations; but she had already gone on to more important matters. "Darling, you wouldn't have anything like a big-brimmed hat around here, would you?" she asked. "Mine just blew off in the convertible. I've miles to drive yet, and the sun does just hateful things to hair-coloring." I found an old straw hat for her. "Well, you're a dream and a darling," she said, trying it on. "I'd probably snatch you away for my own use, if that weren't some kind of incest."

Saying whatever came to her head, she chattered on, trimming the hat with Briney's only necktie, and suddenly remembering she was overdue at some house party down the coast. Only after she had roared off through the field in her long, open car did I realize she had left the straw hat behind.

Mona, our waitress friend, rolled up her eyes when I told her about Tikki's visit. "I'm surprised she didn't forget Brian's perambulator as well," she said.

"Perambulator?"

"The way she keeps him such a child," she said. "He'll probably never grow up now—-just stay a thing of beauty and a boy forever."

Whenever Tikki passed through Laguna after that, she would dart in to say hello, borrow some money, or use the chair-chair, as she called it. I didn't notice that Briney seemed unusually dependent on her, or anyway, no more than she was upon him. She kept him on the phone a lot, and got almost frantic when he wasn't immediately available. "Where is he?" she cried, bursting into the house, one afternoon. "He's not at the hotel, I can't find him anywhere." I explained it was his day off, and he had driven to the airport to pick up Prof Ellison and his wife. "Oh, God," she groaned. "Don't tell me we're back to that."

"Back to what?"

"The college thing," she said. "That old man keeps stirring him up about it. Which is ridiculous, because Briney 'll never go back to school."

I looked at her in surprise. "What makes you think so?"

"Because I know Bri," she said. "He's just like me—always settles for a good time. And—" She shrugged. "—why not? With his good looks?"

The more I saw of Tikki, the more I felt we were on opposite sides, me pulling for the Prof's values, and Tikki defending hers. I never said anything to Briney about it, but sometimes when I suspected his mother might drop by, I simply slipped away to the Sisters.

That's what Briney called the two towering rocks down the

shore from the hotel. They stood close together, interrupting the incoming waves, hurling great sprays of water into the air. Surfers hated them, but I'd sprawl on the sand near- by, and read, scribble in my journal, or sketch. Artists often came to paint here, and the one they called Madge, a gray-haired lady with a tote-bag of watercolor equipment, turned out to be Mrs. Ellison. I realized this one day as I passed the hotel on my way home, and saw her sitting on the terrace beside an old man who had to be the Prof. Briney was standing beside him with a keen expression on his face. "What were you talking about?" I asked later.

"A scholarship to Oberlin," he said. "Prof has this old friend there who could be a terrific help to me if I apply now."

A few days later, I saw Tikki up on the terrace with them, along with her yachtsman and some fashionable ladies in big sun hats. She called to me, and when I went up, could not have been more charming—presented me to her friends and the Ellisons, and urged me to have a glass of iced tea with them. I hesitated, not really wanting to get involved in their undercover tug-of-war; but Briney brought up a chair and sat me right next to the Prof.

The old man quickly put me at ease. He was older than I had thought he would be—his panama hat was a little too large for him now, resting almost on the rims of his glasses—but his voice still crackled with opinion. Briney had mentioned that his passion was the Civil War, so I told him how my Grandfather Nimocks had been wounded in Pickett's Charge at Gettysburg when he was no older than I. As I spoke, my bare legs and arms went all gooseflesh, and the Prof smiled. "I do the same thing," he confided. "I'll mention Shiloh or Appomattox in a lecture, and my flesh will stand up all over my body."

He showed me some of his wife's watercolors. A few were of the shore here, with titles like *Pacific Nocturne # 6*, but most were of the Ohio farmlands. The Prof took great pride in her work. He kept looking at me for my reaction, and I didn't know how to hide it from him. It was not that her paintings were bad—the barns were conventional, if a bit slap-dash, but the silos looming against the sky were nothing short of pornographic. I murmured something about her "fine sense of atmosphere," and passed the pictures on to Tikki's yachtsman. He stared at them with incredulous eyes, then handed them to Tikki, his polite comment drowned out by the sudden uproar of a volleyball game on the beach. Tikki's inspection was quick, but the cheering broke off unexpectedly, leaving her surreptitious opinion for all to hear. "*They look like big dick to me!*"

Maybe it was accidental, but with Tikki, who could tell? The words seemed to echo around the terrace, and she clapped a hand over her mouth like a child. "Oh, what did I *say?*" she giggled.

Briney's face went so red that even his scar seemed suffused. Mrs. Ellison gave an uncertain smile and tried to change the subject, but the Prof stood right up and took the watercolors from Tikki's hand. "I'm very proud of these pictures, Mrs. Barlow," he said. His voice was quiet, but there was no mistaking his estimate of her. "Madge and I grew up in view of just such fields, and I think she has caught them beautifully."

Tikki looked to Briney for help. The Prof's eyes turned to him too. A prayer swept through me that Briney would just let the matter ride. He didn't. Crossing the terrace, he picked up a painting and studied it. "But I can see what Tikki means," he told the Prof lightly. "Freud would flip!"

Then it all disappeared beneath social convention. The guests laughed and began talking again, everyone all at once. Briney went back to passing the iced tea around, and the old man returned to his wife's side, apparently to admire the sun sinking behind the sea. "I think it's cooling off," he told her, after a suitable time. Gracefully, and without haste, they bid everyone good evening, and moved toward the entrance to the lobby. Briney reached it before they did, and held out his hand to help the Prof up the steps. "Oh, I think I can manage alone," the old man said. His tone was affable, but my feeling was that he passed by Briney without quite meeting his eyes.

Some of the volleyball crowd had trouped onto the terrace, and were calling out their orders. "Six beers coming right up," Briney called back, and went into the bar. He didn't return, however, and after a while, I went looking for him.

He was nowhere downstairs. I thought he might have gone up to the Ellison's room to try and repair matters, but when I listened at their door, I didn't hear his voice. Going out to the parking lot, I looked for his old Chevy. It was gone, so I crossed the highway and held out my thumb. Nobody slowed down for me. It was a walk of four miles. Sometimes I found myself running.

Darkness had fallen by the time I reached the plywood house. Briney wasn't inside, although his car was nearby. I kept calling his name, and at last even climbed the hill. He was sitting at the crest, his arms wrapped around his knees, and a slight breeze ruffling his hair. I sat down beside him. In the stillness, I could hear the far-away pound of the surf.

He cleared his throat several times before he finally spoke. "I didn't have any choice," he said. "She's my damn mother, I couldn't just let her sit there, dying."

"I'm sure the Prof knows that," I told him. "He understands."

He popped his lips gloomily. "Probably's packing his bag right now."

"No, don't worry, he'll be back," I insisted. "You'll see. Next summer it'll all be the same as ever."

"The same, yeah," he said, with a little twinge of a smile. "Me, still a bellboy."

Whatever I argued made no difference. He just sat there watching the night and surrendering the dream. In some curious way, I had the feeling he was relieved.

## - 8 -

### AM I BROWN?

Yet the same trap that had caught Briney was set for me.

According to Matt, it had already snapped shut. He joked a bit too often about me being "tied hand and foot by apron strings." It would take an earthquake to shake me loose from home now, he told Miss Brown. What he based this conclusion on was the fact that I hadn't set out on my own after graduating from college, but had blithely moved back with my parents.

It was what most of my crowd did in the 1940's—my friend, Raoul, for instance, still lived with his mother, and he wasn't even young. For me, living at home was just a stopgap until I could finish the novel I was trying to write. However, there is no denying that a year after the manuscript had been sent out (and sent back) I still hadn't gotten around to claiming my independence—had even forgotten I was supposed to. I was having fun, and it didn't hurt anyone. At least, not so long as my family didn't know the precise nature of it. One had to be very careful. *Very* careful! As yet, "out" wasn't in.

And anyway, Matt was in no position to criticize me. Although he fended for himself now, he had been passed around the foster home circuit till he was sixteen and still prized the maternal bond so highly, he was always borrowing a sympathetic older woman to provide it. He called his landlady "Mom," sent flowers to near-strangers on Mother's Day, and especially kept Miss Brown busy—phoned her every morning, brought her little gifts, and gallantly protected her from her own opinion. When she spoke of herself as being an old maid he got indignant. "I don't like you to belittle yourself that way," he said.

"But my dear, it's the truth," she said in surprise. "Saying so doesn't hurt my feelings."

"Well, it hurts mine," he said.

I don't think Miss Brown was prepared for such devotion. She was nearly fifty, an earnest Scot from Edinburgh who, for years, had come to our house every second day to take my dad's dictation. Matt, on the other hand, was blond and handsome, a promising young contract player at Twentieth Century-Fox. "Matt McCall" was the name the studio had given him, and although our affair had not lasted, our friendship had. He continued to drop in on my mother and younger sister, especially when he knew Miss Brown would be there.

"She heard I was testing for a part in *The Green Years* that needed a Highland accent, so she offered to coach me," he explained later. "And then we kept meeting even after I didn't get the stupid role."

"Oh, he would have been really fine in that part, if he had only worked on it," she confided to me once. "But you know how Matt is. He never got around to reading the script—just the lines he was supposed to speak—so he didn't do much with characterization. When I think of it, I could give him such a scold!"

I could not imagine the scold she would give anyone. She always spoke briskly, as if reporting news for the BBC, but at the mere suggestion of controversy, she vanished into efficiency. Accustomed to her reserve, I didn't ask her about this friendship with Matt, but I kidded *him* a little. "What are you going to do?" I asked. "Make an honest woman of her?"

Instead of the laugh I expected, he answered thoughtfully, "She's already the most honest woman I know."

I began to watch this relationship more carefully, perhaps a little protective of Miss Brown myself. She had been an almost invisible part of my life since I was fifteen. While I was away at prep school, I began to notice the initials of a new typist at the bottom of the letters my father wrote to me: MIB. Eventually, little messages from MIB also appeared. "Your father did not get around to signing this," she might say. Or "I enclose a stamped envelope, so you can reply at once." If these postscripts were longer than two lines, she signed them with archaic business formality, "Faithfully, M. I. Brown." The M stood for Muriel, I learned. The second initial was for Isbister, a name new to me then, and still.

She was a bird-boned little woman, whose hair appeared to be dyed with iodine. Actually, it went rather well with her clear blue eyes. When we had lunch out on the patio, she always chose to sit in the shade, for her skin was delicate, and already had that faint pucker special to birthday balloons the day after the party. Generally, she dressed as if for a stroll on the moors—-tweeds, twin-set sweaters, and little brogues—but when she stayed for dinner, she fished a string of tiny pearls out of her purse, and put them on.

All of us were fond of her, but as a family, we kidded each other a lot, and she got her share of this too. I don't think she ever understood it, but she was a good sport. "Right you are!" she'd say to the worst of it. She had no patience with complaint. If a problem couldn't be helped, she consigned it to another lifetime, where things like straight hair or susceptibility to drafts would presumably be readjusted. "Next time around," she would say. To me, generally caught up in some crisis, she offered sound advice, although the British idiom was sometimes startling. "Just keep your pecker up," she urged.

Only once did she allude to her private life, and then indirectly, after Jabot died. It had been her joy to pamper our overweight cocker spaniel bitch; "Wee Jabsy," she called her, with such honied approval that the dog sometimes peed in sheer bliss. She heard the news of Jabot's death stoically, but two days later, while taking dictation, she suddenly pitched forward onto her knees with that kind of wild weeping that almost passes for laughter. "I have nothing," she cried out. "I have nothing! Not husband nor home, and even Jabsy wasn't mine."

My father could do little but kneel there beside her and hold her hand, waiting for the anguished rebellion to pass. As I learned later, he was finally able to remind her she wasn't alone, that she still had her family. Knowing him, he probably meant ourselves; but her answer suggests she had missed this point. "Then what am I doing so far away from them?" she asked, half under her breath.

Possibly that was when the change began. I would find her watching me thoughtfully in the weeks that followed, and sometimes asking odd questions: did living at home satisfy me? was I content? did I feel I'd sold out? She kept asking my father questions too, mostly about investments, and was quick to follow his advice. "The canny Scot, y'know," she would tell him, trying to disguise her seriousness with a wink. "'Put not your trust in money, but your money in trust.'"

It was Matt who eventually told me what she was saving up for. "She's suddenly got it in her head to retire," he said. "Wants to go back to Edinburgh where her sister and brother-in-law still live—take her place in the family, and all that."

Whatever I replied, he interrupted. "It'll just be a big disappointment to her," he asserted. "She'd do a lot better to stay right here in Los Angeles."

"But what's here for her?" I asked.

He laughed in a kind of abashment. "*Me*."

I laughed too, and he picked up on it. "What's so funny about that?" he demanded. "People do take care of each other, y'know."

"Matt, you don't even take care of yourself," I said. He knew this was true. He was making quite decent money at Twentieth just then, had a great wardrobe, and an attractive apartment in Beverly Hills; yet his life had no shape. Most of his time was spent waiting for his agent to phone, or fretting about the breaks he wasn't getting at the studio, and the possibility that his looks wouldn't last. The scotch he turned to for solace wasn't always the canny kind.

"And there's another thing," I added. "Miss Brown's very conventional. I mean *very*! Is she aware that you do a bit of embroidery?"

"I'm not presenting myself to her as a lover, for God's

sake," he exploded."I'm a *friend*! I'm her *confidant*, I'm—" He gestured wildly, distracting attention from the word that must have crossed his mind: her *child!* "Well, I don't care," he continued, mutinously. "I can't let her go."

He dropped by for her after work almost every night now, and sometimes asked me to join them. Increasingly, there were others along too. One of them was Matt's current love, a handsome and affectionate young Mexican dancer named Gaspar. Not that anyone ever called him Gaspar—the inexplicable slant of his eyes had inspired the nickname "Chinguilito." Somehow, he was able to teach Muriel the principle, if not the abandon, of the rhumba. Calvin, too. Cal, a male nurse who took care of my father's elderly cousin, was a big shy boy from Iowa, whose shock of straight brown hair hung diagonally over his brow like a guillotine blade. "Now, all together!" Chingie commanded. "One, and two, and—" While he hummed *Besame Mucho*, Muriel and Cal gingerly waggled.

Before I could escape it, I was part of this closed community. Matt always had something planned for Muriel's entertainment. If there were only four of us, we played cards; five, we went to the movies, and six, he cooked. These were engaging times—-warm, easy-going, full of laughter. I presumed they were a long-standing tradition, but Chingie told me the group had only been meeting since Muriel had decided to go back to Scotland. "It's all part of Matt's scheme," he confided. "He thinks that her belonging to a—y'know—fun group I'll make her decide to stay on in L.A."

"Do you think it 'll work?" I asked.

He shook his head. "She is too—" He giggled, and drew a square with his forefinger.

That's what I thought too. Remaining here as the bosom buddy of a group of young unmarried men was just too unconventional for a fifty-year-old maiden- lady to consider. Possibly Matt came to that conclusion too, for the next time we met for dinner at his apartment, he provided her a more orthodox reason to stay in town: his name was Charlie. Gray-haired and affable, he had been a publicist at Twentieth Century-Fox, and claimed to have discovered Linda Darnell. That was long ago, however, and now he was retired, a widower, and lonely. "But not *that* lonely!" he told Matt after his first evening in Muriel's company.

The most I can say for Matt's matchmaking is that it was well-meaning.

Harold, a lot older than Muriel, took her out to dinner, and called her several times on the phone, but impressed us all as only wanting a free housekeeper. The most disappointing was Duncan, who was the right age, and a one-time Brit; Muriel found lots in common with him, but he was apparently more interested in a quick liaison with Chingie. There were a few more possibilities that Matt invited over before it occurred to him that maybe Muriel wasn't interested in men. Just on chance, he arranged for her to meet Janet from the studio accounting department.

The whole crowd took to her immediately. She tended to take charge, but agreeably, and although her short, waved hair was graying, and her waist beginning to thicken, she had somehow preserved the look of an errant twelve-year-old boy. The night she first joined us, we went to a driving range and sent golf balls flying into a floodlit distance. Janet performed brilliantly, but to our surprise, so did Muriel. "But why is that strange?" she laughed. "After all, where did golf come from? Scotland! Scotland!"

Janet drove her home that night, and Matt held up crossed fingers. When I phoned him at ten, the next day, he had already talked to Janet. "Oh, Brownie's a darling," she told him. "I'm looking forward to seeing her again."

"Yeah, sure, but how did it *work out*?" Matt persisted.

Janet laughed. "Put it this way, honey—she hears the bell ringin', but she doesn't answer the door."

Janet joined us often, that late summer, but the situation didn't change. Nor did Muriel's plans for retiring. In September, on the night before she flew back to Scotland, we met at her rented rooms. They were tiny, neat and nearly anonymous, except for the photographs still on the fake fireplace: an enlarged picture of Jabot, a glossy eight-by-ten studio portrait of Matt, and a blurred little snapshot of her Edinburgh relatives. "All the principals of the drama," Janet whispered.

Over and over, a gramophone kept playing an ancient record that Calvin had brought as appropriate to the occasion—Ethel Waters singing *Am I Blue*?

There was a big platter of the *chilis rellenos* that Chingie had made for a late supper, and Matt had provided a couple of bottles of champagne as a going-away present for Muriel. I watched her in the middle of these friends, suddenly noticing the difference in her. It wasn't just the more kindly color Matt had recommended for her hair, or the less rigid posture Chingie had been helping her adopt. Sitting back in her chair, with her little thimble of scotch, and wholly at rest in the activity that swirled around her, she was downright pretty.

Or maybe I was a little drunk. By midnight, everyone was. Too bright, too brash, too sentimental. By popular demand, Cal stood up and, beaming, stammering, described his famous meeting with Hedy Lamarr at the Hollywood Canteen, back when he was in the army. She would dance with no one but him, and at the evening's end, had looked up at him through her lashes, and suggested he come home with her. It was a soldier's dream, and yet he had blushed and blurted that he couldn't, Captain would be sore if he got back to camp late. Everyone at the party fell apart with laughter, except Chingie, who cried out, "Golly, I'd have gone with her just to see how her house was decorated."

All of us danced with Muriel, and once she was a Muriel sandwich, me on one side of her, Cal on the other. "Am I Blue?" Ethel Waters sang out again. "Am I Blue?" Matt snatched Muriel's little felt hat off a hook, and, tipping it over one eye, strutted across the room. "M. I. Brown?" he sang, in counterpoint. "M. I. Brown?" Miss Brown answered him back, singing out the next stanza in a clear, droll voice. "Was I gay? For a day—?"

It was the first time she had ever given any hint that she knew our secret, and everyone in the room shouted with delight, closing in on her with glasses raised. "Well, I would be, if I could be, boys," she cried. "I've wished, oh, many times, I could live my life as you live yours—-with courage and laughter, daring to be different. Daring, in spite of what people thought. Maybe then, I wouldn't have wasted so many years alone. But—" She lifted up her glass to us. "—maybe next time around! Cheers, dears!"

Cheer we did, and knocked back our drinks, and when Matt spiritedly dashed his glass against the fake fireplace, nobody kidded him for being dramatic

Letters from Muriel began arriving soon after her return to Scotland—long single-spaced typewritten pages that scarcely left room at the end for her customary pledge of fidelity. "Clearly, she's very happy," my mother said. "Her family around her, at last."

I agreed emphatically, glad to have my own preference for home justified. Matt, however, got a different impression from the letters he received. One had to read between the lines, he said. She never included a word of complaint—passed the whole thing off as a joke on herself—but obviously, he said, she had outgrown the nest. For one thing, attitudes that were quite ordinary in California were simply not acceptable in Scotland. The accent and idiom she had brought back from the United States especially offended her brother-in-law. And not entirely behind her back, her nieces called her "the American." Her clothes, even more than her independence, worried the family; seemed inappropriate, even pretentious. "Yesterday, my sister accused me of 'putting on the dog'," she wrote, apparently caught between laughter and astonishment, "and it was just my old navy blue wool."

The build-up of tension became increasingly apparent in subsequent letters, that winter. "If she were anyone else," Matt said, "she'd tell her damn family to stuff it, and get out of there."

"But she won't," I said, maybe to vindicate my own comfortable paralysis.

Matt rushed to telephone me whenever he heard from her, once calling from the set between takes. "Listen to this," he said, and put on a Scottish accent to indicate that he was reading from her letter. "That song keeps running through my head, Matt,' she says here. 'The one you made such fun of at the party. "Am I Brown?" you sang. Or maybe "M. I. Brown?" And I still don't have an answer to that question. Am I—who? Am I what? Certainly not the M. I. Brown I used to be. I'm not even sure she was ever me anyway. Seems as if I have always let other people decide who I was. My mother. My boss. My sister. Even you, dear Matt. But at least learning from you—being who you wanted me to be—has given me the impetus now to dare a little on my own.'"

"What does she mean by that?" I interrupted.

"She's moved out of the family home, and rented a flat in downtown Edinburgh," he told me. "Makes it easier to walk to work, she says."

"What work? She's retired."

"Not any more. She's taken a job with some importing company." His voice rose excitedly. "Don't you see what's happening? Now that she's left her family, and the retirement idea has collapsed, there's really nothing to keep her from coming back to the U.S. and us."

The letter I got a month later told me her employer had asked her if she would be prepared to travel to the Far East twice a year. "Maybe this is my chance to improve on plain old brown, and try for a little sky blue," she wrote, dubiously. "Or even a splash of crimson. But it would mean going to London first, and taking a crash course in Japanese. And the work is much more of a responsibility than I feel capable of taking on. And Japan is so terribly terribly far from home—"

Line by line, I could see her talking herself out of it, giving herself reasons for staying put, exactly the same as I always did. Matt was even more reassuring when I shared the letter with him. Clearly pushing for her return to Los Angeles, he told me not to take this new option too seriously. "She may fool around with the idea of going to Japan," he said, "but when push comes to shove, she'll settle for the tried and true. She always does. After all, this is the gal who still signs even her personal letters, 'Faithfully, M. I. Brown.'"

That's exactly how she signed a birthday card to me, a few months later. But this time it was different. The envelope was postmarked Tokyo.

Her breakthrough stirred me; but not to action. I thought about her example almost every day, but I did not strike out on my own. The bough didn't break, nor the cradle fall. That would take an earthquake, Matt had said.

Within the year, however, my world would be shaken to its very depths.

## - 9 -

## WALK TALL

For the rest of the night, I dozed and nodded, sometimes sitting up in shock, experiencing my arrest all over again. As morning finally came, I took a deep breath and reached for the phone.The only person in Los Angeles who might lend me the money I needed in this crisis was a screenwriter, Ellis St. Joseph; but sleep was dear-bought in his profession, and Nembutal often made it impenetrable. The telephone bell kept ringing—five times, eight times, ten. Even if he heard it, he would make no sudden decision to pick up the receiver. Preparations were needed before he could face the world again: a cigarette would have to be lit, his nearly invisible hair smoothed, and the spirit of Voltaire allowed to descend on him.

I gave up hope eleven times, but on the twelfth ring was reprieved by his Mayfair-flavored drawl. "Hellew?"

Mannered, mandarin, Ellis had been brilliantly successful in Hollywood, and was kindly enough; but his ways were labyrinthine. Even in my desperation, I knew better than to ask him outright for a loan. For him to respond, a request had to come by way of Pisa, Samarkand, and Never-Never Land. Consequently, the story of my arrest, as I told it, was oblique. Soon, he began adding touches of his own—irony and paradox, Grand Guignol horror, and especially, Black Comedy. "You must write about it," he urged. "You can call it, 'The Cock-and-Bull Story'."

I understood that his intention was to neutralize my anxiety with a smile, but I was wet with sweat by the time I hung up. However, by then I had his promise of a loan for a thousand dollars. This accomplished, I braced myself to make the really difficult call. This would be to Jim Holland. His family and mine had been friends ever since we had moved onto June Street back when I was eight. At that time, Jim had been studying law at USC, a jockey-sized young man, forthright, intelligent, and chaste, the kind of role-model that mothers use so ruthlessly on their young. "I'll bet Jim doesn't shirk his homework that way," mine would say. Yet he was more than figuratively a pace-setter. He thought I could be a good hundred-yard sprinter, and for a whole year, had dedicated himself to coaching me for inter-school track meets. I never came in better than third place. "But the next time!" Jim would jubilantly insist. "*Next* time!" He almost made me believe it. I didn't even enjoy running, yet I kept at it to justify his faith in me.

I saw him less often now that I had grown up, too. He was married with children, and a constantly clarifying political future. He came to the phone that morning, with that older-brother manner he had always shown me. "Hey, Bud, what's on your mind?"

I told him straight out. The silence that followed could not have lasted more than a few seconds, but I thought it would never end. "I see," he said. I had heard that tone of voice from him once before, when I had somehow failed him in training. After a moment, he said, "Does your dad know?"

"I wouldn't be bothering you with this, if I'd been able to tell him," I replied.

This too was met by silence. So were my answers to his other questions—perhaps he was jotting down notes. "All right," he said, abruptly. "I'll get back to you as quickly as possible."

I had no appetite when I came downstairs for breakfast. Not wanting to give my parents the impression that anything was wrong, however, I stirred my coffee vigorously, and played with a piece of toast; kept up some kind of conversation, but was deaf to it, listening for the telephone in the next room. When it finally rang, I made a show of answering it casually. Jim's voice was subdued. He had been in touch with some of his contacts at City Hall, trying to get the charge against me reduced to a mere violation. I had apparently been too honest about myself at the station house the night before, however, and as a result, the authorities were firm about me being tried as charged.

I began to sweat again, desperately needing to ask questions, but unable to risk being overheard in the breakfast room. Somehow I crowded all my uncertainties into one cryptic word. "*When*?"

"Are you asking when you will be tried?"

"*Yes.*"

"I'm getting your hearing postponed for a few weeks," he said. "Your lawyer will need time."

Again, I strained to keep my side of the conversation noncommittal. "*Haven't got one*."

"Haven't got a lawyer?"

"*Don't even know any.*"

Understanding my need for secrecy, he said carefully, "I'll try to arrange for a friend of mine to see you at his office between appointments this morning. Could you be there by ten?"

Even though I had to reclaim my car, and pick up a check from Ellis, I was at that office before ten. The lawyer, whose name was Button, maybe Bouton, turned out to be a cheerful, graying man, with family photographs mixed in with the diplomas and civic citations on his wall. He spoke quickly, confidently, though I didn't always understand the legal terminology even when he explained it. He did say that my arrest stank of entrapment, a questionable police tradition which he despised. "With any luck," he added, "we can get the case thrown out of court."

"And if we can't?" I asked.

He smiled. "Let's cross that river when we come to it."

But that river had been sweeping the earth from under my feet for hours, and I needed to know the worst: could I be sentenced to jail?

"Anything can happen," he said. "In a court trial, believe me, *anything* can happen."

I returned home to wait on developments. "Keep a low profile," Jim cautioned. "Don't—*gallivant.*" I didn't need to be told. The usual fun and games had no allure for me now; I was already absorbed by full-time hiding. "A terrible thing has happened," I wrote in my journal, but that lone sentence was my last entry in the book for several years. At first, I escaped into sleep whenever possible, but soon began writing compulsively. I had been at work on a predictably autobiographical first novel, but now put it away, and lost myself instead in writing about the cut-throat intrigues of a family in Lyons, France, a place I had never been, in an era long preceding my birth. It was fiction at its most fictitious, but at least it took me far away from my own experience.

Oddly, in the midst of this self-imposed blindness, a new range of vision began to develop. The rambling California hacienda we lived in was an instance: I had merely made use of its convenience and comfort since my return from college, but now, threatened by the possibility of prison, I found myself homesick for it in advance. Unasked and without a vestige of skill, I began taking on some responsibility for the house—chinked up cracks in its adobe walls, found a solution for our perpetually wet cellar, got up early in the morning to climb the plum trees and harvest the ripe fruit.

This rediscovery of my home included my parents. My father especially had lost my attention. A calm, instructive man, something of a prophet in his field of economics, he had chosen to be black velvet to my mother's diamond, forever providing a backing where her warmth and enthusiasm could shine. I had seldom stayed home at night, but now spent my evenings with them, playing cards, reminiscing, or helping prepare the plums for the thick, delicious jam which was a joint family endeavor. As I began to enjoy their company again, I found that the bond was very different than it had been during my childhood. They had been responsible for me then, and now, for the first time, I began feeling responsible for them. A pressure was building in me, a promise to myself that they would not be hurt by all this.

Almost immediately, this newfound determination was put to the test. My lawyer's plan to fight the issue of police entrapment seemed straightforward and high-minded, showing every possibility of clearing me. It seemed something quite else to the subtle mind of my screenwriter friend. Ellis invited me to lunch at an obscure restaurant that suited his sense of intrigue. "You realize, don't you," he said, "that by fighting the entrapment, you'll be challenging one of the L.A. police department's most profitable operations. Of course they'll fight it! Rather noisily, I should imagine."

"What makes you think so?"

"I have sources," he said. The lift of his almost indiscernible eyebrows suggested he had been in touch with authority too important to divulge. "With no trouble at all, the Los Angeles police could come up with testimony that would suggest you'd practically raped that poor innocent plainclothesman," he went on. "The sort of messy testimony that gets picked up by the less finicky newspapers. Not that your family would be likely to read one, but it would only be a matter of time until word wafted around—"

I scoffed at him, but as he kept touching on the same nerve, I began looking for alternatives less risky. From Ellis' point of view, the solution was simple. "Have your lawyer plead you guilty," he advised. "Pay the fine, and forget it."

"Great! But if I'm sentenced to jail?"

He answered loftily. "It's your lawyer's job to see that doesn't happen." My lawyer didn't want the job at all, if we weren't going to face the issue of police entrapment. "Get yourself a vag-lewd expert," he said, as he showed me to the door. "They're used to pitching in the towel." I had no sooner gotten home than Jim Holland phoned—I was making a great mistake, he said. If I pled guilty, as charged, the fact would always be on my record. I told him that wouldn't make any difference, I would never be running for Congress.

"Maybe not," he said, "but it leaves you wide open to blackmail. And God help you if this country ever elects a Hitler. You'll go right into the gas chamber."

I recognized the validity of this, but it did not change my mind, and the next day, I met with a lawyer who specialized in my kind of case. Not a distinguished jurist like Mr. Button, I was warned, but nonetheless, shrewd and sure. Case-hardened, unsmiling, he looked like a lower-echelon actor's agent, and spoke in a curious blend of legalese and private idiom. Never once, for instance, did he mention homosexuality by name. He called it "queerdom." And his first advice to me was far from Blackstone's finer points of law. "Get the curl out of your hair."

"It doesn't go away, I'm afraid."

"Then cut it off!"

His further advice had the sound of an order: I was to get myself a job at once. I explained I already had one, that I was a writer. "I'm talking about a real job," he interrupted. "I've got to make you look like you do something useful."

I took part-time work in the stockroom of a large department store on Wilshire Boulevard. It was poorly paid, and menial, but not uninteresting, and it left half the day free to work on my book. Meanwhile, my new lawyer got my hearing postponed again; and then, before that date could arrive, had it postponed yet another time. It was the rotation of judges he was waiting on, holding out for the most propitious. This was all-important, he said: a judge without charity for 'queers' —and that included most of them—could spell disaster for me.

This continuing delay only left me more time to picture what could go wrong, wiping out any equanimity I had left. Let the damn hearing happen, I kept thinking. Get it over with! Even if they hanged me, it couldn't be worse than, day after day, trying to square my foot to a constantly shifting floor. It did not help that my parents had begun to know something was wrong. My loss of weight was one clue, and at first, my mother read it as unhappiness in love. Impulsively, and out of context, she put her hand on mine, and urged me to send the girl some flowers.

My father neither offered solutions nor asked questions, but there was something in his manner that suggested his intuition was not confined to the Dow-Jones. I had begun to run out of money, and could not even buy a present for my younger sister's birthday. "It's all right," she said. "I understand." But did she? I prayed not. Too many people already knew. Ellis, for all his help, had not been able to keep from leaking the story to his friends at the studio. "Ah, yes," said an English actor, when we were introduced. "You're the lad who—"

And if gossip could not be contained, much less could chance. One Sunday after church, my family and I stopped for lunch at the Pig'n'Whistle, a long time favorite along Hollywood Boulevard. Midway through the meal, I became aware of two couples finishing up their lunch several tables away from ours. One of the men was in his late twenties, well-built, with a fresh complexion, and the look of an ex-sailor. My scalp began to tighten, and I kept sneaking uneasy glances in his direction. I could not be sure it was not the decoy cop who had arrested me.

As he and his party got up to leave, he caught me watching.

Perhaps he assumed I was someone he knew. Or if he actually was the detective, he may *h*ave recognized me. In any case, he cut across the room towards me. Unable to breathe, much less to think, I stood up and faced him. As he started to speak, I interrupted: "*How've you been?*" One wrong word now could strike the set in mid-scene. "Great," he said. We shook hands, and then, nodding to my parents and sister, he moved along. "Who was that?" my mother asked. "I'm not sure," I said.

But what I was not sure of was my ability to control the unforeseeable anymore. The only way to protect my family from some chance exposure was to clear out. For the first time, I faced the necessity of leaving home. The ideal would be to move to Chicago or New York, far enough away so that my letters home could present me as the son they believed they had, without hard evidence to the contrary. Until I was free to leave town, however, it seemed wise to take a room in the Valley or at the beach, and pass it off with the excuse that I really needed "to get some writing done, undisturbed."

As it turned out, my time was already up. Even as I began to look for garage apartments, I got a call from my lawyer confirming the date of my hearing. I was as ready as I would ever be; and yet, when that morning came and I arrived at the courtroom, I felt that familiar self-induced stupor creep over me, dulling all my responses. I sat there trying to breathe regularly, dressed soberly, and with my hair shorn almost to my scalp. As the chamber filled, I saw Jim Holland come in and sit down, his eyes never turning toward me. I looked over my shoulder several times to see if, by some chance, my father was there. He was not, and that, at least, was comfort. Then the judge entered, and the stout little clerk chanted a medieval song that began *Oyez, oyez—*

I waited in a kind of suspended cognizance until my name was called. My lawyer nodded for me to come forward. Obeying, I lifted unblinking eyes to the judge. The charge against me was probably read, and there must have been discussion between him and my lawyer, yet all I recall now is his voice asking how I pled, and the other voice, my own, answering "Guilty". Forever after, I heard him sentence me to a year in prison, and then, in the same impersonal voice, suspend it. I was smartly fined, however, and put on probation for twelve months before the knock of the gavel closed the case.

Some kind of reality began to return as I left the courtroom. I glimpsed Jim in the crowded corridor, and we walked along, side by side, neither looking at the other. "What will you do now?" he asked at last.

I told him of my plan to go to New York when my probation was over, but that seemed no solution at all to him. As we reached the street, he met my eyes for the first time. "Bud, could you change?"

I said as gently as possible, "Probably not."

"But would you try?" he asked. "Would you make every possible effort?"

To satisfy him, I said I would. We shook hands, and I understood that our goodbye was likely to be forever. When he had gone, I stood there a moment longer. The downtown air was poisoned with traffic fumes, but I breathed it in gratefully—filled my lungs. Then I headed on home.

## - 10 -

## BLUE HEAVEN

At the end of her letter, just before she signed *love, Marty*, she wrote, "I'm suddenly afraid of the direction I'm heading, but I don't know how to turn back anymore." It was the first time she had volunteered even this much information about her personal life. However, by this time, I was pretty sure the lover she was talking about was a girl.

We had been corresponding fairly regularly in the year since we had graduated from college. That in itself was odd, since we'd never been close on campus. She had sat across the room from me in English 107, a slender girl with a cool, level glance, and long eyelashes that were repeated in shadow on her cheeks. She seldom participated in class discussion, although when she silently disagreed with someone's opinion, a quickening pulse in her throat contradicted that appearance of cool. Once, after I'd read a paper aloud, she had slipped me a note after class. "Beautiful," it said. Always hungry for approval, I kept it in my wallet until the word rubbed away.

Eventually, I asked her out to a movie—asked her twice, in fact, but she was always busy. As far as I know, she never dated anyone on campus—word had gone around that she was engaged to someone in nearby Orlando. If this were true, she never brought him to the dances or the games. The one time I saw her away from class was when I happened into one of those "happy hour" bars along the highway, and she was sitting in a booth with some young woman. She seemed not to see me, and yet that sudden pulsing in her throat suggested she was uncomfortably aware of my presence.

I was too busy answering questions about my own life to wonder much about Marty's. I would have probably forgotten about her, except that just before graduation, she let me read some poems she had written. I was expecting regulation moonwash, but found instead a passionate outcry, intense, original, moving. On impulse, I sent them to Edith Haggard, a New York literary agent, who had been able to sell a story of mine to *Esquire*. Although she eventually sent the poems back, her letter of rejection transported Marty. "Some of this is just wonderful," Haggard wrote. "A haunting voice. But unfortunately, poetry won't pay the rent on my office—"

Even when graduation scattered us, me back to Los Angeles, she home to Galveston, we kept in touch, trading enthusiasms about books, authors, and each other's work. Sometimes, I tried to coax a little personal news from her as well, but she never picked up on this. Not until this last letter. And before I could even reply, she wrote me another, still more revealing for all its ambiguity.

"You and I have never discussed it in so many words," she wrote, "but we have always sensed the truth about each other. Alas, I am far more comfortable with the truth about you than about me. I don't want this kind of life for myself. I see nothing in it for me but unhappiness. Yet I am more and more drawn into it. Do you do this too? Fear, but follow?"

A few months earlier, I would have probably dashed off a reassuring letter, telling her to come on in, the water's fine. But since then, the water had cooled, and I myself was in it way over my head. I was serving my year's probation now, and nothing crossed my path that I did not instantly interpret as a police set-up. Some young man had only to give me an interested glance, and an alarm went off in my head, jangling until I rushed away. On every side, an unbearable pressure was put on me to change my life; but nobody had any suggestion about how change was possible. I was in Marty's boat, seeing nothing but disaster ahead, not knowing how to turn back, and unable even to reach out to anyone for comfort.

And so the letter I wrote back to her simply continued to chat about books and the new plays. She didn't answer it. She didn't answer the next two either. It wasn't until some months later that I learned she had taken a razor blade and slashed one of her wrists. Not that she ever told me. I had to hear of the attempt from someone who didn't like her much, or me at all. "And the laugh is," our mutual critic confided, "the person she wanted to die for is a real dog's lunch. Some dreary woman who runs a secretarial service—"

I telephoned Marty at once. Neither of us could get the words out when we heard the other's voice. And in fact, we never did speak of my arrest or her suicide attempt. She had been ill, she told me, but was feeling fine now. "Except," she added, hiding behind a droll voice, "I've got to get away from here soon, or I'll die."

"Where'll you go?"

"New York, I suppose. That's where people go, isn't it?"

"That's where I'm going," I told her. "Soon as I can find the money."

"Are you poor, just now?"

My troubles had left me in economic chaos. "Pretty poor," I said.

"Find someone to share expenses with," she advised. Then she laughed. "Maybe you and I should live together."

It was a joke, of course. Yet we kept joking this way over the next few months, and gradually it began to seem like common sense. Each of us had come to a violent stand-still in our lives, and neither wanted to risk going back to the old way. Maybe two paralytics giving each other support could manage a few steps forward.

Discussions of budget began to replace literary matters in our letters. Plans were made, discarded, revived. Marty would take part-time work once we got to the City. So would I, if the proceeds from selling my car evaporated before I could finish my novel. Yet as our enthusiasm grew, so did our doubts. A telegram from Marty, one Sunday night, put things succinctly: *It will never work.* I telegraphed back just one word and an exclamation point: *Quitter!* By the next letter, she was once more discussing where we would live. "In Greenwich Village, if that's not too cliché," she wrote. "But not a cold-water flat, let's promise ourselves that—a hot tub every night is my one surviving pleasure in life."

Marty went to New York in July, and somehow found an apartment for us, plus part-time secretarial work for herself at *Redbook.* As my probation had another month to go, I did not join her until mid-August, arriving in the middle of a relentless heat wave. She met my train, and despite the damp cotton dress, and hair pasted in wet commas on her brow, she managed to sustain that cool look. We kissed the air in front of each other to avoid sticking together. It was almost too hot to talk, but going downtown on the subway, she said, "You're going to kill me."

"Why?" I kept myself from looking at her left wrist.

"The apartment I rented for us," she said.

"Is it terrible?"

"Eye of the beholder," she said.

We got off at Sheridan Square, and walked west toward the river. Here the buildings had increasingly a penitent air. Marty drew out a key as we approached a narrow white house on Greenwich Street. Our names were already written in a slot beside our doorbell, but they had a parvenu look next to the stately identification printed just above us: Squire Fairfield. "I haven't met him yet," Marty said glibly, to distract my attention from the crumbling plaster and cracked paint, "but we'll have him down for tea soon."

Three flights of stairs led us up to our apartment. The living room doubled as a bedroom, and there was a kitchenette and booth-sized bathroom. The tub itself was in the kitchen, with something like a cellar door covering it, so it could also be used as a table. Lots of light came streaming in through the front windows, but this was promptly absorbed by the flat, horizonless blue painted on every wall, door, and ceiling. An old tune came back to me, and I sang out, "—just Molly and me/ tee da da da dee/ We're happy in my blue heaven—-"

She thought I was making fun of the place. "You hate it, don't you?"

But I didn't. Contentment began to seem possible to me for the first time in months. "It's going to be the greatest," I told her.

Her smile was tentative. "You haven't tried the beds yet."

There were two of them, though they were not twin. One was a double-size cot with a thin mattress on its curled wire web. Across the room from it, flush with the wall, was a single bed whose box spring said *pung!* when I sat on it. We tossed a coin, and I got the cot. "We can always rig some kind of screen between us, if it'll make you feel safer," I told her.

"I don't think we need worry about that," she said, with gentle irony. "We're not each other's type."

Not all our problems were resolved that simply. Or that honestly. In our first month in the blue apartment, we were so eager to make a go of living together, we didn't complain about anything, no matter how troublesome. I cooked the dinners on alternate nights for five weeks before she suggested that, henceforth, she do all the cooking. I never did have the heart to tell her she was no better cook than I. My concoctions may have been primitive, but at least scorch was a recognizable flavor. Her food simply confused the taste buds, an example being orange jello in which asparagus had been sunk.

Money also kept us teetering on the brink of disaster. Every time I was our banker, she made me feel I was a miser, begrudging her even the necessities of life; and when she handled our expenses, I had the constant impression she was flinging our money to the wind. I cut a picture of Marie Antoinette out of *Time Magazine*, and pasted it on the bathroom mirror. It was gone by mid-morning, and expenses continued to soar, except that she never served cake again.

Our major problem was partying. Neither of us was particularly social. We had no acquaintances in the neighborhood, and I didn't want to re-connect with the people I knew uptown. Yet we didn't need to know anyone to run with a group in the Village—merely to touch toe to the current was to be swept along. A couple we met in the check-out line at the market asked us to drop by for a drink at their loft, and before anyone had even gotten our names straight—they called *me* Marty, and *her*, Jess —we were rushing about with the downtown loud-crowd.

I never learned most of their names either. One young man was known simply as "the boy who shat in Auden's tub," an achievement which apparently opened doors to him the length of Manhattan Island. We went to a party on Thompson Street, where a girl sitting on the sill of an open window started laughing and fell backwards onto the courtyard four stories below. She was dead when the ambulance arrived, and they couldn't find out who she was, as someone had pinched her purse during the excitement. On the romantic side, we went to a wedding breakfast at the San Remo Restaurant, where the groom was Eugene O'Neill's younger son. Too many toasts soon sent him stumbling into the men's room, and when he didn't return, the bride asked me to go see if he was all right. "I'll be out in a minute," he growled, when I tapped at the stall door, under which the feet of two people could be seen.

Marty and I kept waking up with hangovers. She missed going to work twice, and neither of us was getting any writing done. A quarrel about nothing kept lurking, never actually happening, but not letting us relax either. "It's not working out, is it?" she sighed, at last.

"How can it work out?" I cried. "We're both rushing right back into the same life we were so frantic to get away from."

She had a way of drawing herself up by merely lifting her eyebrows. "I am not rushing back."

"That girl in the army fatigues, who was eating you up with her eyes, last night?"

"I can't help what other people do with their eyes," she said. "I didn't even notice her."

Yet she knew I was telling the truth, and I could tell it made her uneasy by the way she fumbled her hand over her wrist. She said nothing more then, but after dinner that night, instead of ironing the sprigged cotton she wore for social occasions, she conspicuously curled up on her bed and began reading. "The fact is, I hate parties," she said, abruptly. "I only put up with them because I was afraid you'd get bored staying home all the time."

We did stay home more often after that, though never all the time. We went to Loew's Voluptuous (as she called it) for double-feature movies when we could afford it, and to the zoo when we couldn't. I enjoyed being seen with Marty—she held herself beautifully, her head was well-shaped, and her nose joined her brow in a straight line, like the goddess on a silver dollar. She wore practically no make-up, except for the Vaseline she smeared on those long eyelashes. I think she was pleased with the way I looked too, tall and lean, usually wearing levis. Sometimes she called me "Tex" to tease me. For the same reason, I would call her by her real name, which she hated: Martha.

Once again, our writing became the focus of our lives, Marty biting her pencil and frowning at a pad of yellow paper in the living room, me rattling away at my typewriter in the kitchen. A gray cat, finding the lights on and the windows open, came in to live with us, almost invisible against our blue walls. We got to know some of our neighbors. Squire Fairfield turned out to be two elderly women on the top floor, nurses from the first World War. Miss Fairfield was senile now, and seldom left her bed, but Miss Squire still churned with vitality. "The man who read the meter today asked if he could use my 'terlet'," she told us. "I said, 'Hell, honey, you can pee up the chimney, if you'll just say Myrna Loy for me!'" He did, pronouncing it Brooklyn style, Moina Ler, to Squire's whooping delight.

The perfect autumn merged into a less perfect winter, but the heat pipes thumped reassuringly, we had a Christmas tree trimmed with popcorn, and the first time it snowed, Marty, born and bred on the warm Gulf Coast, ran outside, wheeling round and round, her arms flung out and her head thrown back, sticking her tongue out to taste the drifting white flakes.

Yet somehow it wasn't enough. All our pluses kept adding up to a minus. Even with each other's constant company, both of us were lonely. "It's not working, is it?" Marty asked again.

I probably thought she was blaming me for the fact, and that cut my temper short. "If it's been such a bust, why bother to stay?"

She lifted her chin. "Because it's my apartment," she pointed out. "But don't let that bother you, I'll go at once, if that's what you want so badly."

"Good!" I shouted, and both of us began packing our suitcases.

Except I didn't want to go, and she didn't either. Instead, we looked for ways to compensate for not being who or what the other was missing. I typed up her poems for her, she cut my hair for me, and both of us picked up each other's clothes. What we never quite did was to level with each other. After six months together, I still had to guess what she was thinking. She never openly confided, even when she was in pain. The February chill seemed constantly to seek out the scar on her wrist. It was no more than a little pink line under her watchband by now, but these twinges apparently kept alive all those images she couldn't live with. Though she never spoke of them, I would hear her whimpering in her sleep at night, and sometimes when she sobbed aloud, I would find myself stumbling across the cold room to wake her up. "C'mon, baby, it's just a dream!"

It never seemed like a dream to her. Even when her eyes opened, she would cling to me, her voice still fragmented with fear or despair: "She didn't care, she stood right there, laughing at me—"

"Who did?"

"Lundy! Lundy!"

"Who's Lundy?"

A long pause. "No one," she finally said.

Sometimes when she didn't settle down to sleep again, I would climb in beside her and we'd share a cigarette, or I'd rub her back. Our voices were low, gradually becoming drowsy and disconnected, already part dream. "—can't find the tray—"

I roused slightly. "What?"

"I know I had it," she explained sleepily. "I put it on the elephant shelf—"

Usually, I wandered back to my own bed before morning, but sometimes I only dreamed I did. And sometimes, when we lay so close together in those hours before light, pretending sleep so we wouldn't have to explain, we encouraged the impossible to happen. "Crossing the glass bridge," she described it, later. It didn't happen a lot, and was in no way to be confused with sensual curiosity, or just snuggling close to keep warm. At heart, it was the desperation of both of us to go straight. Sometimes we were successful, and sometimes we weren't, but the darkness was on our side, and we were silent even between ourselves, except for the husky acceleration of our breathing.

On those mornings when we woke up still together, we

acted as if nothing had happened. Yet the unspoken made itself heard in other ways. We found ourselves beginning to relax, even to assume that we were a perfectly usual, normal young couple. I would hear her singing to herself with cheerful banality,"'—just Molly and me/ tee da da da dee/ We're happy in my blue—'"

Many of the boundaries that separated us grew less distinct. Her bureau drawers and mine gradually became the same, we finished each other's sentences, and shared the same tube of toothpaste. One Sunday morning, we even sat in bed, drinking sherry from teacups, and openly discussing our sexuality. She admitted she had tried to alter her direction once before, when she was fourteen, by "letting the boy next door." In turn, she wanted to know how many girls I had slept with. Two or three was the fact, but I told her ten. "And didn't you enjoy it with them?" she asked, defensive for all womankind.

"Well, sure I did," I told her. "Girls can be terrific fun. But as the feller says, 'They're not like the *real thing*.'"

She wanted to know the difference I found between men and women. "Not anatomically," she added quickly.

I frowned thoughtfully, clearly a world-authority on this subject: women were probably more emotionally satisfying, I said, but men more exciting.

She made a face at her teacup. "You'd find women more exciting if you knew how to excite them," she said. "Most men don't have the foggiest notion. I'm told that half the time, they rush right by it."

"Right by what?"

"The key to the city," she said. "The boy in the boat."

"*Who?*"

Her smile was mysterious, but for once she spoke out plainly. I had never heard of the clitoris before, although my fraternity brothers at college had spelled out everything they had discovered in the course of intensive investigation. "But maybe they didn't know about it either," Marty said. "After all, it takes a woman to know what pleases a woman."

We learned lots of things from each other, that spring. Yet coincident with this, we began to find costs we had never anticipated—odd little instances of possessiveness, subtle shows of jealousy. These appeared, faded, and took shape again, like the gray cat blending in and out of sight against our blue walls. In April, it suddenly leapt out into full view, when Mary Sullivan, my longtime playmate from the Waldorf-Astoria book shop, finally tracked me down. "Why don't you get a telephone?" she cried. "I've been trying to reach you for months."

Mary never met anyone she didn't like, and had an immediate hug for Marty. Her house-warming presents were quickly put to use—she emptied the pint of whiskey into glasses, passed around the bargain fruit, and cleared a place on our bureau for the photograph of herself in black tie at a costume ball. "Everyone was there, darling," she told me. "Everyone we know."

She chattered on vivaciously, scattering names I had almost forgotten, evoking the kind of hectic fun that was her specialty. Only after a while did I become aware of Marty's smoldering silence. Her eyes fired up every time Mary said *we*. I called her on it when our guest left. "Well, you were just as bad," Marty cried. "Hovering over us, like you were afraid she and I would like each other better than we do you."

"Hovering!" I cried. "The hell I did!"

"The hell you didn't!"

I expect we got rather noisy about it, because the people downstairs began tapping their ceiling with a broomstick. Worse, she hit me, and I hurled one of her shoes out the window. I was repentant the next day, and when she got home from work, I had some jonquils for her on our bathtub table. She in turn gave me a new typewriter ribbon, and to prove she wasn't even remotely possessive, brought a big-eyed young man from her office, and left us alone while she fixed coffee. I was touched by her generosity, but only the typewriter ribbon was ever put to use.

Things never did get any less complex for Marty and me.

"Molly and me," I almost said. And probably should add, as the song does, "and baby makes three." Whether she actually got pregnant, I still don't know for sure. Marty, being Marty, kept it all to herself. In retrospect, however, I realize she and I hadn't been particularly careful in our midnight happenstance—*consequences* was still the most obscure word in gay vocabularies. On that morning in June, when everything started falling apart, the most important thing on my mind was our decision to paint over our gloomy blue walls. We had just finished stirring up the pigment when she faltered and laid down her brush. "I'm simply not sure this is what I want," she said, as if to herself.

I thought she was talking about the new color, just an ordinary off-white we had decided upon earlier. She gazed over my shoulder for a long time, however, and then lay down on her bed, murmuring that the paint fumes had given her a headache. During the afternoon, she went upstairs to borrow an aspirin from Miss Squire.

When she hadn't returned by dinner, I climbed up to the top floor. The old nurse had her lying down with a white cloth on her brow, and was fanning her. "Touch of the flu," Miss Squire said crisply. She saw me looking at the wicker suitcase of potions and pills lying open and plundered on the floor. "I've given her some medicine," she explained. "Strong old-time stuff, but she'll be ship-shape tomorrow."

Actually, it was over two weeks before Marty was herself again. But in a sense, she never again was the Marty I knew. If it had been a miscarriage rather than flu, or if Miss Squire's old-time pills had terminated a pregnancy, I do not know, but it's no play on words to say something had gone out of Marty. Maybe what she had lost was the far-out hope that going straight would set her life right. More and more often now, I found her gazing out of the window at nothing. The poems she had spent so many hours working on were put away, nothing left of them but the tense look she got when a line wouldn't scan. I could still get her to smile sometimes, and once in a while, to laugh, but when she woke up in despair at night, she no longer turned to me for comfort.

I began to look behind her explanations when she started coming home from work late. "There was no way to let you know in advance," she'd say. We still had no telephone, and whenever she had to call her parents in Galveston, it meant going several blocks to the Rexall drugstore. Lately, she had felt the impulse to talk to them often, and sometimes was gone for an hour. One night, I followed her. She didn't stop at any Rexall drugstore. Where she stopped was a handsome brownstone on West Tenth Street. When she disappeared inside, I waited a moment, then went into the foyer, and checked the nameplates of the tenants. A temporary card said Lundy, as somehow I knew it would.

It didn't matter to me. I told myself so, several times. It was to be expected, the same with me as with her—high time for each of us to stop hiding, and get back to our real lives. On the way home, I circled Sheridan Square once or twice, then resolutely sat down on a bench. A choice was available: a student from the campus at Washington Square pretending to read under a streetlight, and on a bench near mine, a blond young man lazily patting his pockets for a match, always a good come-on. I ended up with neither of them. A cop was pacing up and down in front of the little Square. He wasn't watching me, or them either, and yet his presence under these circumstances triggered a reaction over which I had no control. Even as my heart began to hammer, I got up and hastened away.

My flight seemed foolish by the time I got back to the apartment. Just as foolish, but not as quickly acknowledged, was my resentment of Marty for snapping out of her nightmare while I was still trapped in mine. I pretended to be sleeping when she came in, shortly after; and might as well have been asleep when we saw each other the next day. We didn't really talk at all until late the third night, when I woke up to find her sitting on the edge of my bed. "Can I crawl in?" she whispered.

I moved over. "We've been so silent lately," she continued, when she lay beside me, "and what I wanted to tell you is, I do care for you."

I wasn't very receptive. "Yeah?"

She nodded. "Maybe it doesn't always look that way, but I do. I think we both do. We love each other a little. It's just that we're not—y'know—*in*."

"In?"

"In love. But that's all right, isn't it? *In* isn't what I want anymore. It hasn't ever made me happy. *In* is what I cut my wrist with. But caring, like you and I do —not owning each other, not hurting each other—that's what I want most now."

She had never spoken this openly to me, and some kind of embarrassment robbed me of what I wanted to tell her. Only as she was about to get out of bed was I able to blurt, "What about *her*?"

She turned back. "Lundy?"

I nodded.

"Yes, I've seen her," she admitted. "But really *seen* her, this time. Seen through that whole obsessive thing. It's—" She took a deep breath. "—out of my system for good."

"Then—you won't be moving out?"

"I won't be going anywhere," she promised.

But two days later, she had vanished, and Lundy too.

## - 11 -

## THE SECURITY GOD

I knew the risk, but after all, I wasn't really following him—merely going in the same direction. He strode down lower Fifth Avenue, then turned at Eighth Street, and went into the Tip-Top diner. I continued on my way, walking clear to Sixth Avenue before I decided to have another cup of coffee after all. Returning to the Tip-Top, I sat down at the counter next to him and ordered. Even to my own ears, my voice sounded funny.

I was too wise to look at him directly, but whenever I could, I sneaked a glance at his reflection in the mirror behind the counter. He was about thirty-three, but had kept the look that distinguished tramp athletes at college. He didn't talk like a college man, however, so it was probably just the result of wearing chinos instead of denims, and cropping his hair short. His sleeves were rolled up for work, and disclosed a tattoo on his forearm. It would have been easy to ask him to pass the sugar, and springboard this into a conversation. But I couldn't. I didn't try to scrape acquaintance with good-looking strangers anymore. I'd had one surprise too many.

He finished his breakfast before I did, and stood up. "Take care, Elsie," he called to the waitress. I glimpsed the tip he left her by his saucer.

The waitress, a tall stick-shaped woman with tightly rolled curls, saw it too and suddenly showed a crowd of teeth. "Aw, you didn't have to do that, Harree."

He smiled at her gravely, and went to the door. "See you tomorrow." This was revealing—his seriousness, his generosity, and especially the fact that he would be back the next day. Not that this mattered, since I had no plan of carrying it any further. Even so, I found myself using tricks to find out who he was. "That guy who just left," I said to Elsie. "Isn't that Harry Nowak? Used to be with Con-Edison?"

Her accent was pure New Yorkese. "Naw, that's Harry Shaugnessy, he's a coppenter. Moonlights as a security god."

I liked the image of this—a god of security! And by moonlight! The picture stayed with me all day, and teased me back to the Tip-Top for breakfast the next morning. Yet neither then, nor on subsequent days, was I able to break through my inhibition.

I was less guarded with the other regulars at the diner, however, and managed to ease out some more information about him. He had been in the army. He was separated from his wife. He was troubled with headaches, and Elsie kept aspirin in the cash register for him. She had a crush on him, but not everyone else was so admiring. The short-order cook dismissed him as an oddball. And possibly Harry was a bit odd—most of the people I was drawn to were. That way, I didn't stand out so glaringly myself.

Sometimes I'd see him on the street. Once, I brushed by him in the hardware store. Other people had no trouble approaching him. Bums and beggars made a bee-line for him. I was impressed by his patience and willingness with them. Even when he had no money to give, he seemed to reimburse them with his attention. I used to try to imitate this manner—would confront myself in the mirror when I was shaving, and speak as straightforwardly to my reflection as he did to the beggars. "If I had any dough, just now," he'd tell them, "I'd sure as hell shoot it to you."

Bit by bit, I put together a pretty clear picture of Harry. It was myself who remained unknown. I had grown more and more withdrawn, especially after Marty had moved out of our blue apartment. When loneliness finally got too much for me, I moved across the Village to a brownstone on University Place, where I was more likely to meet people. My one-room apartment was elegant in a dilapidated way—marble fireplace that didn't work, and tall casement windows stuck shut—but the loneliness persisted. Sometimes, in desperation, I went to the bars on nearby Eighth Street— Mary's and the Old Colony—but if anyone spoke to me, that obsessive fear of being entrapped by police decoys returned, and I left. My funds were dwindling fast now, and unwilling to ask my family for a loan, I spent longer hours each day at my typewriter trying to get my novel finished. The few people I saw were elderly. My landladies, the Misses Emma and Harriet Mittelstaedt, had me in for tea occasionally. And sometimes I went to Number One Fifth Avenue to visit the illustrator, Majeska, whom my agent had introduced me to. Her color plates for the books of Isak Dinesen were moody and haunted, intricate as cobwebs, but she herself was resolutely down to earth. Born Henrietta Stern some seventy years before, she spoke in a flat Philadelphia voice, and even when she had guests, continued to paint in bed undistracted. "How old are you?" she demanded one night, not looking up from her work.

"Twenty-five."

"And it doesn't bother you that you're wasting your youth?" she asked, bluntly. "Always by yourself, always alone."

I tried to pass it off as a joke. "It's safer."

"How do you mean?" she asked, peering at me now through her gold Harlequin glasses. "How do you mean, *safer*?"

For an instant, I longed to tell her and get it out in the open—the shame at having been arrested, the dread of it happening again. Yet not even the promise of sympathy or relief could make me speak of it. Not to her, not to anyone.

"Whatever it is, I wish you'd snap out of it," she continued. "You're beginning to look old and sound paranoid. Kick over a trace or two, for God's sake! Get out in the fresh air, meet someone your own age."

If I had known how to, I would have. Instead, I kept on as I was, half-prisoner, half-guard. My irresolute attempt to cultivate Harry was as far as I seemed able to go. But that was before I cut through Washington Square after a late movie one night. The paths were dark there, and lovers strolled together, or searched for each other as yet unfound. It was always a temptation to slow down, and at least *see* who was there. But I never did—the hurried footfall of a policeman reminded me why. He paid no attention to me, but swung by as if going for help. I sensed tension and alarm, even before I saw Harry hastening toward me. He was carrying someone, the body slackly outstretched across his arms, and as he strode by, he must have recognized me, for he said curtly, "Get his sack."

Thinking there had been an accident, I quickened my pace, and found a knapsack lying overturned by a bench. Snatching it up, I ran back along the path, and caught up with Harry just as he cut across the lawn and pushed into a clump of bushes. Paying no attention to me, he laid the body down on the ground.

The body sat up uncertainly. It was a young black man, Watusi-tall and visibly disoriented. When he tried to stand, his long legs buckled, and he sprawled forward helplessly. "Take it easy," Harry whispered, and held him down. Scraping together a pile of dead leaves with his free hand, he heaped them over the black man's body. "Don't move," he warned. Then he headed back to the path, running bent over.

I did the same. We reached the street about the time the policeman, flanked by another, marched into the Square and up the path. "They won't find him," Harry whispered with satisfaction.

"What happened?" I asked.

"Some poor junkie," he said. "Too doped up to run off when the cop went for back-up. So I hid him."

"Someone you know?" I asked. He shook his head. "Then why bother?"

"Well, hell!" His eyes met mine sharply. "Think I was goin' to leave him there for the Law?"

I thought about it all the way home—lay in bed for a long time, wondering. It was more than his put-down of the police that intrigued me. I was too insecure to believe in anything but ulterior motives, yet I wanted to think that some kind of compassion for the damned really existed. In view of Harry's attitude toward beggars, his gallantry to gawky Elsie, and this unassuming kindness to the cokehead, he seemed to me an odd blend of Don Quixote, St. Francis, and Mr. America.

Finding him in the Tip-Top the next morning, I sat down beside him and said hello, just as if that were something I had always done before. He gave me a wink to acknowledge that we had shared some mischief the night before, though he didn't seem much interested in hashing it over again. The past had passed—a new idea for me—and he was much more interested in what was happening today. On that morning, and the ones following, I found myself discussing things with him that had never particularly interested me before: the pennant, City Hall, Belmont. He liked the track, and once we went there together

—I even won a few dollars. Another day, he turned up with two little girls in plaid parochial jumpers, nieces of his, he said, whom he was taking to the zoo in Central Park. I tagged along. One Sunday, he and I took Elsie down to the Battery, and looked out over the water to the Statue of Liberty. I teased her because she was so moved by the experience. Harry smiled at me kind of shame-facedly, and showed me his bare arm. It was all goose-bumps.

I could scarcely believe the way my life was opening up again. The journal I kept began to spill over with conversations with Harry, and descriptions of where we went, what we did. In re-reading it now, I seemed especially surprised that it was not just me seeking him out, but him so often reaching out to me. It was his seeming approval that I could not quite figure. I kept asking myself if it was merely the same consideration he showed all the other misfits, or was he somehow attracted to me? I could not really believe this last. It felt too much like wishful thinking. He looked so straight. That wedding ring on his finger seemed such a final statement, even though I knew he was separated from his wife. He mentioned her a few times. She lived in Jersey, he said, and they had a nine-year-old girl. He was frank about everything, yet I always ended up not knowing what I wanted to know.

My uncertainty about him came to a startling head on the day he asked me to help him with a job in Brooklyn. "It's a long ride, and not much pay, but we'll split even, okay?"

I had to laugh. I would have gone to China with him for nothing.

At nine, that morning, we were on the rooftop of an old building in view of the Bridge, demolishing some ancient pigeon coops. Half the time, I wasn't even sure what I was doing, but Harry seemed to know for both of us. Even when we got too busy to talk, we enjoyed the camaraderie of working together. Nostrils pinched, eyes mere slits, we pried old timbers loose and stacked them, rolled up jagged lengths of chicken wire, and swept clouds of powdered bird droppings into the brisk seaward breeze.

We had finished the job by noon, but were unrecognizable. Dust and flecks of fluff covered our faces and bodies, except where sweat had streaked us. Harry had a key to the super's apartment, and we went down to wash up. The place was empty, and the blinds pulled down. It was the first time he and I had ever been alone in private, and involuntary thoughts stirred in me, at once lazy and aggressive.

Harry had already flicked on the light in the bathroom. The shower there was scarcely more than a tin closet. He turned the faucet on to get the hot water activated in advance, and then began undressing. An unexpected little warning reached up my spine and into the roots of my hair. "C'mon," he said. "Get your clothes off." I started to tug my T-shirt off, and then didn't. There was something a little too pat about all this. It was somehow too good to be true—reminded me of the too-easy access that had led to my arrest two years before. A frequency far fainter than sound cautioned me that Harry was, after all, a security guard, and for all I knew, had the authority to arrest. I sneaked another glance at him. He did not look remotely threatening, but then, neither had the fresh-faced stud on Hollywood Boulevard, who had made himself so available and then flashed his badge.

Perhaps Harry saw me falter, for, grinning, he reached over and tweaked my T-shirt. "Let's go, man," he said, and got in the shower.

I backed away, yet I could not look away. Under the rush of water, his body was magnificent. Muscular. Masculine. The face and throat were day-laborer tan, and so were his arms up to the biceps. The rest of him, chest, butt, and thighs, were startlingly white. There were work scars still whiter on his shoulders and shanks, and the soap froth around his gender seemed whitest of all. In addition to the name Marie tattooed on his forearm, I could make out a faded blue panther just above his knee. "One tattoo may be intriguing," my friend Ellis had once noted, "but two are a warning."

And warning seemed all around now, dense and dissembling as the steam that had begun to fill the bathroom. The powerful figure in the shower dimmed out of view, then faded in again, the same way my suspicion was doing. I kept trumping up reasons why I had to be wrong about him. If he was really an undercover cop, why would he have hidden the junkie from the law? But the question was already engulfed by the answer: that whole scene in Washington Square had been a set-up, a deliberate scheme to get me to trust him, and then when I was at ease with him, to let me incriminate myself. Even if our bodies so much as touched by accident—and how could they fail to, in that cramped little shower stall?—he would have all the evidence he needed to arrest me. "And the next time, you won't get off so easy," I had been warned.

"Hey, c'mon, boy, get in here," Harry called.

Sweat or condensation was sliding down into my eyes, blinding me, and the inside seam of my trousers was strangling me. "I'll meet you downstairs," I gasped. Stumbling out into the hall, I raced down the five flights to the street.

When I was out in the fresh air again, and the pounding of my heart began to subside, my relief at having escaped gradually settled into the realization that there probably had been nothing to escape from. Rather than relief, I felt a sharper dismay at having made a fool of myself in front of Harry.

I had managed to clean up a little when he finally came out the front door, "Hey, what happened to you?" he cried.

"I got too hot," I blurted. And then, in case this could be misinterpreted, added lamely, "The steam."

He must have known it was a lie, but he made nothing of it; kidded me a little, read the baseball scores over somebody's shoulder on the subway, and treated me to lunch at the Tip-Top. His uncritical acceptance made me so ashamed of my distrust, I swore it would never happen again.

But it did. Several times. The worst was on a drive to Yonkers to return a truck he had borrowed. It was late at night, with the radio music and drizzle of rain seeming to cut us off from the rest of the world, isolating us together in the cab. Conversation gradually fell away. Our knees were side by side, not quite touching, but when he shifted the heavy gears, his elbow traced a light arabesque on my arm, as if by accident. "Give me a drag of that," he said, when I lit a cigarette. I held it to his mouth, able to feel the supple contraction of his lips as he sucked in the smoke. Moment by moment, a recklessness I had nearly forgotten was waking up and flexing in me, a feeling I had learned to distrust, but found almost impossible to hold back now. Yet it was not my recklessness that swerved us into such sudden chaos. Behind me, and far away in the night, I could hear the thin quaver of a police siren.

It drew nearer, louder. Uncomfortably, I edged away from Harry. I had not even touched him, I reminded myself. Maybe my intention was unlawful, but nobody could prove anything. In spite of this, my breath grew short. I began to picture the speeding police car forcing us over to the side of the road, and Harry, cool-eyed now, whipping out his badge and telling me I was under arrest. By the time the screaming, flashing vehicle actually did cut in behind us, my courage and self-control were so undermined that I lashed out at him accusingly. *"Okay, you can stop acting now, your friends are here!"*

He veered the truck onto the shoulder of the road, and an ambulance shot by us. In the swiftly disappearing dazzle of its light, I could see Harry's anxious scrutiny. "What do you mean?" he asked. I had no answer for him—squeezed my eyes shut, turned my head away.

He asked me again when we were returning to Manhattan on the subway. "I'm just tired," I told him. "I'll get some rest tonight." But I didn't. I lay in bed wide awake, unable to shake the feelings of distrust and betrayal. I gave myself every argument, made fun of my fears, and told myself that nothing so absurd as this suspicion was going to ruin my bond with Harry. And yet, even as I was saying so, the decision to pull back from him seemed to have been made without my consent. I caught a little sleep towards morning, but while it was only eight o'clock when I awoke, I felt it was too late to meet him for breakfast. And the day following, when I started off to the Tip-Top, I somehow ended up at the Copper Kettle.

He telephoned me around noon that day. "Hey, where've you been?" I told him I was sick in bed. He asked, "Want me to come sit with you?" But I gave him some excuse. All I wanted now was to be left alone.

I found my old solitude waiting just where I had left it. I visited my old ladies, I kept my journal every day, I worked on my novel. Around ten o'clock at night, I'd wash up and go out for a drink, usually to a tavern near Fourteenth Street that catered to workmen and serious drinkers. As I recall, I never spoke to anyone there—just sat at the bar stolidly putting it away. And sitting there at the bar, one night, probably feeling sorry for myself, and already a little drunk, I saw Harry come in the door.

I could tell he'd had a few drinks, himself, and knew he was looking for me by the way his eyes circled the room. When he saw me at the bar, he came over and sat down beside me—ordered a drink, and gave it a gulp when he got it. "How come I don't see you anymore?" he asked, in that straightforward way of his. "I do something wrong?"

I pretended to discover him now. "Well, well, well, if it isn't Officer Shaugnessy!" I said, full of bourbon and bravado. "Is it a ticket to one of the policeman's balls yer wantin' to sell me? Or if that sounds too racy, how about an invite to a cop supper?" The sudden alarm I showed was fake. "Did I say 'cop supper'?"

"Yes."

I pretended relief. "I was afraid I'd said 'cop *sucker*' and broken some kind of law."

He frowned. "What's got into you?"

I didn't want to answer, or even intend to, but the words had piled up inside me these last ten days, and suddenly I was saying them, a wild rush of them, all the suspicion and fear and frustration that had been tormenting me for too long. I mocked him as a low cop spy, and bounced his treachery and sick persistence back in his teeth.

He neither took offense, nor laughed in my face, but studied me as if adding up all these twos and twos, trying to make them equal four. Somehow they did. "You been in trouble with the Law?" he asked.

I gave him some more heavy-handed sass. "Now what gives you a *queer* idea like that?"

"Because I been there, myself," he said. "Did the same thing after I got out: kept thinking people were trying to railroad me back to the slam."

But I didn't believe him. I stood up to go, but he went right on talking. He had been arrested for bumming across Georgia when he was twenty, he said. The punishment he took, the humiliation and contempt, belittled everything I had gone through. His first night in the county jail, some prisoners had ganged up and raped him. "They didn't even use spit to get in me," he said. "I found out, that first week, the only way to keep this from happening regular was to let one of those bastards have rights to me in return for protection. That's how it was done there. And before I was done with that jail, I was doing the same for a younger guy."

Maybe his story was even true, but I was no longer in any state to know. Torn between wanting to believe him, and being afraid to, I was in such turmoil that being sick to my stomach was only the outward sign. I took a couple of frantic steps toward the fresh air, but didn't get there on my own.

He must have grabbed me up and hauled me out, because the image I got in my confusion was being carried like the black junkie in the Square. I found myself bending over a curb, with him holding me steady for the next spasm of vomiting. "Move on!" he told some gawkers in his security guard voice. When I was able to stand alone, I twisted free of him, and headed down University Place. He was still behind me when I reached my door. The high flight of stairs in the front hall tipped radically to one side even when I was sober, and when I couldn't negotiate it, he steadied me up to the third floor. Inside my apartment, he put me under the shower, or tried to. I gave him some more resistance, and it finally got him sore. "What gives, for God's sake?" he demanded. "Even after all that, you still think I'm the Law?"

"I don't know what you are!" I cried.

"Well, let me make it plain," he said. Holding me still, he put his mouth on mine, open and wet. Then he slid it down. I didn't need a lot more proof.

When I awoke at five that morning, he was still lying in bed beside me, naked now, and asleep with his arm thrown half over me. Next time I drifted around, it was seven, and he was gone. However, he phoned about three o'clock, and after work came over with a paper bag of hamburgers and a change of clothes. I won't say he moved in, but during the next six months, he lived at my place a lot more than he did his own.

Our relationship wasn't going to be forever—we both knew at the onset that eventually he would go back to his wife and daughter—but while it lasted, we made the most of being together, using each other's eyes for perspective, and exchanging our gifts. I taught him to type with more than one finger, and filled in some of his education. He got my windows so they would finally slide open, and built me some handsome bookshelves. There was another kind of building going on, too: I still could not speak of my apprehension by the police; but with Harry's patient encouragement, I gradually stopped arresting myself every time I wanted to make love.

I only became aware of this change the first time I got lonely after Harry went back to his own life. I was walking across Washington Square when I saw a young man with a nice smile coming toward me. Eventually we got talking, and he asked if I lived around there. I told him, "About two minutes away."

"Like to have some company?" he asked.

I said I'd love it.

# PART TWO

Bill Butler

## - 12 -

## BILL, COLLECTED

The face that I shaved every day seemed the same, and yet there were changes—I was getting older. "Maturing is the better word," Bill told me on my thirty-third birthday. Any show of sympathy from him was rare, and came so unexpectedly, it is best described as an *attack* of cordiality "You'll finally begin to relax and enjoy," he added, in this same celebrant tone. "Part One of your life was all self. With any luck, Part Two is going to be other people"

Bill, himself, lived in a world of "other people." Actors mostly do; but a writer's life—or anyway, *this* writer's life—is too often solitary. Every day, I sat at my desk, alone in my apartment, copying down my characters' conversations, sorting over their memories, intensifying their conflicts. After dark, I had a quick dinner, then toured the gay bars. This, however, did not make for a satisfying life—tricks leave little trace. It had not occurred to me yet that I might be looking in the wrong place for the kind of companionship that shapes your life—the sort of friendship I was to discover at last with Agnes or Gar. With Marion. With Joe, Margery, Eddie. Even, I suppose, with Bill.

Bill Butler. Nothing really bound him and me together but cussedness and a little low comedy. People assumed we were lovers, but the mere idea made us whoop with laughter. This wasn't especially flattering to the other, but then, flattery never played much part in our long and precarious association. I never threw away any of the letters he wrote to me, but there were months, even years, when we didn't speak.

We had met in the eleventh grade at Cumnock, a small academy in Los Angeles, where I had been enrolled after a stormy refusal to go back to prep school. Bill was the student assigned to show me around that first day, but the single glance we exchanged seemed to sober us both: he was shortish, and I, the self-conscious reverse. What little attention he paid me after this introduction seemed designed to cut me down to size. I tried to keep up with him as he strode through the halls, but missed most of the information he flung back over his shoulder. After too many minutes of this, I slipped away for a cigarette, and he didn't come looking for me.

We managed to avoid each other until nearly Christmas, when both of us were cast in the school's annual English comedy. I played a butler, and Bill's role was not much better. Everyone agreed he was the best actor in school, but despite blond hair and ceaseless vigor, he never got to play leading roles. His slouch and pallor forever typecast him as Banquo's ghost, and such.

Still he turned out to be hilarious as the old Vicar. According to him, I was quite funny too, although unintentionally. I pretended not to hear his put-downs, but when New Years Eve came, I threw a party as a pretext for not inviting him. It was not a particularly good party, but it improved in the days following as everyone discussed it openly in front of him. "What'd you do on New Year's?" someone asked him. He could have easily invented something, but answered with a kind of bitter pride, "I had a glass of tap water at twelve, and said to hell with it."

Somehow, this refusal to save face touched off a turn-coat sympathy in me —a suspicion that underneath his unbearable brashness, he was alone and desperate. This was something I knew about, myself, and I began to wonder if it sprang from the same secret cause.

We ran into each other coming out of a movie, a week later. The film, *Winterset,* had been dismissed by the critics, but I had loved it, and got noisily protective about it before Bill could tear it apart. Except he turned out to have loved it too. We stood talking at the bus stop, and heaped so much scorn on the critics, we had none left for each other. The next day in gym class, we found further things to agree on: George Gershwin, Picasso, and almost any movie star. He seemed to have no life of his own—never mentioned friends or family, and I got the feeling he was an orphan. When I asked, he let out a wild bray of laughter. He had perfectly good parents in Kansas, he said, but there was no money, and he had left home to get his education as best he could.

I had nothing against education, but he was a kook for it—waited tables in the school dining room to pay for his tuition, and after class, took odd jobs like washing windows at a Hollywood hat shoppe. This was no chore since it was his peephole into the show-business world he dreamed about. The hats there were high-styled, but low-priced, and attracted studio people, even some of the great stars. One of them, Carole Lombard, would groan as if mortally seized when she saw a hat she liked. "Aw, honey," she moaned, trying it on, "this one's a cocksucker!" Bill would not be persuaded that less spectacular people still winced at strong language. He repeated the story even in the housemother's hearing. "Why shouldn't I?" he demanded, when I called him on it. "*It happened!*"

He was unwilling to compromise on anything, including traffic. When he got a ticket for jay-walking, I cut class to go downtown with him and be moral support when he paid his fine. School work paled beside such adventure, and soon we were slipping off downtown every spare moment. We discovered Peniel Hall on the seedier side of Main Street, where drum, tambourine, and trumpet summoned the bums to repentance. We sneaked backstage at the Philharmonic Auditorium while *Aida* was being set up, and wandered through the empty dressing rooms, trying out the singers' throat sprays and reading their fan mail. We rode ten blocks past our bus stop, eavesdropping on a remarkably plain woman as she unbosomed herself to a friend. "—he said to me, 'Vera,' he said, 'Vera, you're not just desirable, you're temptation itself—'" Vera, which she pronounced Vee-ra, spoke penetratingly through her nose, but it was her facial contortion that held us hypnotized. She kept every feature going as she spoke, licking her teeth, sucking her cheeks, and twisting her mouth into ever more precise enunciation. She became a part of our daily life—the mere stretch of the lips or mention of her name was enough to transform an ordinary remark into instant wit. We began to see her everywhere: on the street, at the movies, in the classroom. Reduced to Veras, the world was nothing to be afraid of.

We took to calling each other "old sport" with just enough bite in it to hide any approval. Neither of us had ever had such a good audience before, but along with this reward, there were penalties. At his best, Bill had the high spirits of a touring player, but it was equalized by his most trying feature, a relentless Midwestern honesty. To his mind, even tact was a form of lying, and all too often, he felt compelled to point out whatever truth was least convenient. "Let's do something about that complexion, sport," he would say airily. "Polka dots aren't in."

For all his compulsive honesty, and the insults we exchanged in the name of candor, we were cautious about letting each other know too much. Sexual orientation, for instance. In those clandestine days, a misplaced trust could ruin your standing at school, and even jeopardize your eventual acceptance by a college. So we had exhausted sidestep and indirection by the time I asked him outright, "Are you queer?"

"Naturally," he said, without a blink. "And everyone knows you are too."

"They don't know any such thing!" I protested.

"If they don't," he snapped, "they probably think the Empire State Building's the Eiffel Tower."

This came too quickly for logic to validate, and we stood there trying to glare at each other. Then both of us collapsed in helpless laughter. My laugh was loud, but his deafened dogs. And it was this kind of laughter, irrational, uninhibited, and usually directed at ourselves, that made our patience with each other last as long as it did.

America's entrance into the second war waited until we graduated from college. Although conscience kept urging us to take our part in this great global struggle, the armed services were sending out loud noises about how straight they intended to keep the ranks. The slightest deviation would be hunted down and punished, we kept hearing. "If you're caught, it could mean court martial, disgrace, and even prison," an older friend warned us. He had already declared himself, and his draft card was marked 4F. "Think of your family," he urged. "Spare them the humiliation."

My arrest on the morals charge having already disqualified me, I did not enlist, and assumed Bill would decide against going too; but nobody ever made up his mind for him. When those greetings from the government finally arrived, he stored his clothes in my family's attic, and made himself ready for induction. My mother and dad gave him a farewell party—twice, in fact, once when he came back on leave. Basic training had not automatically transformed him into a soldier—the olive drab uniform and army haircut merely made him look miscast. But ready or not, he was shipped out.

The letters he fired from Europe broke every rule against sending explosives through the mail. Their very salutations seemed to detonate. He could not or would not adapt himself to army life, and with that holy commitment to speaking his mind, he attacked everything from the Supreme Commander to government-issue underwear. It was not just the Military's incompetence, waste, and graft that he raged at, but the heaped-up hype used to justify it. "I'm tired of Days of Infamy," he wrote, on the anniversary of Pearl Harbor. "I'm ready to celebrate a day of *Famy*— something that civilized people can observe. Which is why I have decided henceforth to commemorate December 7$^{th}$ as Bette Davis Day."

It worsened after he got to see some action overseas. He seemed to have decided that if the Army would not conform to his standards of excellence, he would simply wash his hands of it, and ignore the war entirely. Consequently, he filled up his letters with gossip about events and personalities far from the world conflagration —events and personalities, in fact, that did not exist anywhere. "Went to the most amusing party at

BooBoo, Duchess of Blackpool's," he wrote. "It set the Smart Set right on their Cannes. She had the chorus line from *La Bore Crashing* flown in to entertain us during cocktails, and after din-din, introduced the most divine redneck preacher, who made us all leap up and confess our sins. Except I couldn't think of any of my own, so I confessed several of yours."

There were pages of inside revelation about the cowboy star, Buck Weinstein, and his horse, Schlepper, ("—they're not speaking just now.") and full reportage of the Dallas Palace Little Theatre's all-woman *Life with Father.* But gradually, his letters became the trans-Atlantic edition of *The Muses' Loot.* This too was pure invention, slender folios of really terrible verse, edited by the imitable Mrs. Tremble McKinley Haynes, and featuring, among many other lyric voices, the poems of Flower Bungley Basset, the Sweet Singer of Coldwater, Michigan. "Mrs. Bassett's *Jazz Phantasmagoria* is too well-known to need our mention," he editorialized, "but, reader, who can resist quoting its final lines, so pregnant with meaning for today's mad youth?

'Go on, flapper, your way wend,
Life will get you in the end.'"

It was a curious departure for a young man so furiously committed to speaking the truth; but perhaps absurdity was the only note left to a voice already hoarse with protest. When I finally wrote to him demanding that he either report what the hell was going on over there, or to stop writing to me at all, his answer by return mail confined itself to a single word, *routine*, but repeated seventy-five times. This ended with advice to go fuck myself, followed by a six weeks' silence.

Resuming our correspondence took effort and a slice of humble pie: I submitted a sheaf of really blank verse to the editor of *The Muses Loot.* "Mrs. Tremble McKinley Haynes thanks you for your splendidly lyric vision," he wrote back benignly. "So does our Mrs. Bassett. So does our newest contributor, a friend of yore and a friend of yours, the unforgettable, nay, immortal, Vera."

By the time the war was over and Bill returned to the United States, I had moved to New York, and was living on University Place in Greenwich Village. "What gives with this town?" he demanded over the phone, the day he disembarked. "It's dirty and deafening and ought to be replaced immediately." We met for a drink at the Astor Bar. Whatever he may have felt about his stint in the army, it had accomplished wonders in transforming his appearance. He was as good as handsome, standing a lot straighter, with his blond hair cropped short, and his face so tan that the eyes blazed blue as gas flame. However, it was the same old Bill when it came to blurting out what was on his mind. "Oh, God!" he groaned, when I suggested he stay on in New York and share expenses. "We'd strangle each other in ten hours."

Somewhat to my relief, he took the train back to Los Angeles the next night. A month and three letters later, he was back in Manhattan, climbing the lopsided stairs to my small apartment. There was nothing for him on the West Coast, he explained. He knew no one there anymore, and besides, Hollywood was no place for an actor.

Once he had moved in, the apartment shrank a size smaller each day. Bill's energy had the surge of rush-hour traffic, and even when I persuaded my landladies, the Misses Mittelstaedt, to rent us an adjoining room, I kept feeling that a four-lane highway had been routed through the place. Within a week, he was holding down two part-time jobs—three, if you counted volunteer work for a national theatre organization. In between times, he made the rounds of Broadway producers. I kept imagining him bursting into their offices, just as he did when he came home at night. "Okay, okay, okay!" he would cry. "Everyone off their butts, let's see some action here!"

In a way, it was what I had been missing. After a long day of working alone, it was good to break for dinner with someone, and sit across a table, laughing and talking nonsense. Yet even this relaxation got lashed by tempest, once Bill managed to land the lead in a modest Off-Broadway production of *Hamlet*. Every night when we met at some spaghetti joint after his rehearsal, he would ruin his digestion and mine by acting out the day's ordeal. He had studied the role since kindergarten, to hear him talk, but the stage director, whom he always referred to as T.U.T. (That Utter Turd), was refusing to abide by this superior knowledge. The dueling that resulted between them was not confined to the ramparts of Elsinore, and only ended with a *coup de grace* from the critics, whose faint praise closed the show.

Apparently untouched by this disappointment, he plunged into any work he could find. It was providential that Miss Emma Mittelstaedt, the elder of our landladies, should die just then, and we helped move the dusty contents of her antique shop up to the apartment she had shared with her sister. Here, the knick-knacks and what-nots waited, piled up and unsorted, like artifacts in a crypt. Only a wall separated Miss Harriet's quarters from ours, and late at night, we could hear her wandering through those heaped-high rooms, grieving, sometimes singing a few notes of a song her sister had loved. "Spooky," Bill said; but when she went for a week's rest at her relatives', he was ready. Recruiting me, he worked open her spring-lock door with a plastic collar-tab, and we sneaked into her dim, airless parlor. It took two days just to hide the junkier bric-a-brac—fringed lampshades, dusty bead flowers, and a really tacky papier mache bust of King Tut. Even then, the rooms looked haunted, so we re-painted the walls, re-upholstered her armchair, and washed all the windows. When Miss Harriet came home, Sunday night, her fluttering cries of rapture pierced the walls like shrapnel. "Oh, boys, what a wonderful— How can I ever thank— What can I do to repay you?"

"Well, if you could spare it," Bill said, modestly, "I'd like that *unusual* bust of King Tut—" ( He sent it as a token of his regard to T.U.T.)

This had been the first time he and I had ever worked

together harmoniously, and we tried it again the next year, when Bill heard that Gian-Carlo Menotti was looking for someone to assist him during the rehearsal of his latest opera, *The Consul.* Bill's experience with this medium was limited to having been quartered at the great opera house at Wiesbaden during the war. He couldn't even read music. However, in two nights of grueling study, he let me teach him how. Whistling Puccini, he met the composer and nailed the job.

This was Bill's breakthrough into important theatre, but in many ways it was a disappointment to him and an ordeal for everyone else. He would not compromise. To safeguard Menotti's work, he tolerated no shortcuts or excuses—in rehearsal, tangled with tenors, wardrobe women, and Union representatives. "Even with me," said Menotti, a darkly handsome falcon of a man. "To insist always on perfection is—" His shoulders heaved. "—a terrible burden for all."

*Tell* me! I thought. At long last, my novel had been accepted by a publisher, and one day, I asked Bill to take some galley proofs back to my editor on his way to rehearsal. On the subway, he checked over my spelling, which was always fallible. Then, since he was at it, he re-structured my grammar, improved the vocabulary, and reinstated the kind of comma-crazy punctuation that Henry James had rejoiced in. "Just suggestions," he explained later; but the suggestions were in eradicable red ink, and when he handed them in, my editor was furious. "On whose authority did you make these changes?" he fumed.

"The Queen of England's," Bill retorted crushingly. "It's *her* language!"

There was always a certain grandeur in his inability to process his opinions. This really flowered after the prestigeous Joshua Logan decided to direct a play I had written, and we were suddenly lifted into a sphere of sensitive egos. At a party honoring Sir John Gielgud, I overheard Bill telling the great actor that he had walked out on his *Hamlet*. John, the kindest of men, did not take offense, but I did, and on the way home, told

Bill off. He defended himself fiercely. "Somebody's got to tell the truth in this business," he cried. "Otherwise we'll lose our whole basis for acting and writing."

"Uh-huh," I said dryly. "Yeah, Bill, sure."

He faced me indignantly. "Do you think I only said I didn't like John's performance because my own *Hamlet* failed?"

"It certainly crossed my mind," I said.

He marched on, disgusted by my cynicism. When we got home, he pulled out the manila envelope of reviews that had carped at his performance, and, to show me that truth works both ways, underlined in blue pencil all the critics' negative opinions and mailed them at once to Sir John.

If such Olympian integrity was difficult to live up to, it was nearly impossible to live with. Tension kept accumulating between us as time passed, and the occasions for shouting at each other multiplied. Bill's threat of moving out began to occur more often; and yet, when we weren't arguing, we still made each other laugh. And there was something else too—by some mad fluke, even against our wills, we had come to depend on each other.

Still, good times, bad times, all detonated when Josh Logan phoned to say he had no further plans to direct my play. The disappointment was crushing, and I took to my bed, unwilling to even think about it. Two days of this was enough for Bill. "Oh, for Christ's sake," he burst out, "face up to things for once!"

I put a pillow over my head. He snatched it away. "You always do this," he persisted. "Hide away from anything unpleasant."

I sat up furiously. "So do you!"

"When did I? Just name once I ever did!"

"All the time! You hide every day of your life, you're scared shitless that people 'll find out you're queer."

"All of us are scared of that! You're scared, yourself!"

"And all during the war too! " I yelled. " When you couldn't handle the pressure over there, you hid away with games and high camp! *The Muses Loot,* for God's sake! Flower Bungley

Bassett! *Vera!*"

That really burned him. "At least *I* went to war" he shouted. "I served! You took the easy way out. Declared yourself! Pulled the pillow over your head!"

His voice was too penetrating, and the bronze ashtray by my bed too handy. I slung it at him, deflecting my aim at the last instant, so it hit the fireplace instead, taking a chunk out of the marble. For a moment, our eyes met, shocked, incredulous. Then he slammed out of the room.

He took an apartment of his own only seven blocks away, not a Siberian distance even by New York standards, but it was nearly a year before we ran into each other again. Both of us were polite, even pleasant, but this meeting did not lead to another. Mutual friends kept us abreast of each other's careers. He sent congratulations when I got a job as an assistant to my idol, Elia Kazan, but his own job with Menotti had not lasted—he had finally been a shade too outspoken. However, the experience had propelled him toward musical theatre, and eventually he was staging productions for the Metropolitan Opera. When the Met presented a new opera for which Bill had provided the libretto, I showed up to applaud. He had done the same for me, coming to the out-of-town opening of my play, *A Swim in the Sea,* which Hal Prince had produced. His project did not have a much longer life than mine. We were both sympathetic when the other's work failed, but remained coolly distant if it had even partial success. When we met at a cocktail party, Bill, now known by the more dignified name of Henry, was looking very *maestro* in a silvering beard and a cape. He asked after my mother, whom he had always been fond of. She had been dead for three years, and I was shocked to realize how long it had been since he and I had last spoken.

And it was quite a few years more before we spoke again. Not because we were still feuding; we just weren't in the same part of the world at the same time. Bill's familiar candor having alarmed Sir Rudolph Bing, head of the Met, he spent more of his time in Europe now, staging operas, teaching singers to act, managing music festivals. Surprisingly, he sometimes sent postcards from Rome or Graz, or even Texas. "*Boheme* again, bitch soprano, new *ami*, marvelous weather." And always, at the end of the message, a stylish exhortation, "Thrive!"

But was he himself thriving? I had no way of knowing anymore. Curiously, it was my younger sister who put me on his track again. Unknown to me, she had kept up a correspondence with him over the years, and she phoned me now in concern. "He hasn't been well, and now I can't get hold of him at all," she said. "His answering machine breaks off in the middle with an awful sound, and there's no way to leave a message."

I called his number, and had the same experience. I phoned again the next day, thinking the problem would surely be fixed by then. It wasn't. Nor was it any different on the third day. At last I went over to his address to check out the situation, and learned he had had a heart attack, and was at Roosevelt Hospital. "He has a phone by his bed," my informant said, "but if you call, don't be upset."

I did call, and I was upset. His voice was faint, and betrayed no interest in me, himself, or the world. I asked if I could come see him. "It wouldn't be convenient," he whispered, and hung up.

I shrugged, and told myself I didn't give a damn anyway. So the next day, I went to see him.

It was a mistake. He was gaunt and pale, and his eyes, unwelcoming. "I told you I didn't want to see you," he whispered.

I replied in our old mock-insulting way, "Then you should've begged me to come. I'd have stayed away."

He would have turned from me, but the nearly invisible tubes taped to his face, arms, and body, didn't allow him much freedom. He closed his eyes so that at least he needn't see me seeing him.

I sat down beside the bed, searching for something to say. It wasn't easy. The past was too hurtful to discuss, the future too uncertain, and we no longer had any mutual friends to dish. I babbled along about the weather and the traffic. It wasn't very interesting, but that made no difference since he wasn't listening.

It was a reprieve when the nurse came in. "Now, how's our patient today?" she cried. The stretch of her smile laid bare her long teeth, and tightened the cords in her throat. "Are we ready to have our temperature took?"

Both of us stared at her. The way the woman's urgent enunciation made her face writhe had been familiar to us for years. We sneaked a look at each other, and simultaneously mouthed her name. *Vera!*

I had risen to go, but now sat down again, and when she was gone, picked up the conversation where we had left off years before. "A fireman on Delancy Street has been giving her a very hard time," I confided.

Bill's voice, worn down to a whisper, was exactly right for stirring up scandal. "Tell me every word!"

We gossiped about Vera and the fireman in complete absorption, this leading into a discussion of the Dallas Palace Little Theatre's latest production, a life of Bess Truman acted by computers.

I saw him the next afternoon, and the next. On the day he was allowed to sit up, he handed me a worked-over sheet of paper. The writing was hard to make out, looking like a forgery of his usual hand. "Out loud," he whispered. I cleared my throat, and read it back to him: *Elvis Elegy* by Flower Bungley Bassett.

"Pink-pout punk, pot-
Hot. Husky hero heroin
Secedes his star, slides slow his moon
And high the holy handsome heaves—"

"She'll finish writing it tomorrow," Bill croaked. "The same four lines, except backwards, it'll make a statement for our time."

I did not really expect Bill to recover, but he did. I swore I would not lose track of him again, but I have. I don't doubt that he's somewhere in Paris or Santa Fe, bossing prima donnas around and menacing stagehands. Any day now, I expect to get a picture postcard, or find a note in a bottle washed up on the shore. "*Rigoletto* again," it will say. "Loathsome tenor, but the chorus is piquant, and (one of them) affectionate." And at the end of the message, of course, "*Thrive!*"

You too, sport.

## - 13 -

## WHAT CAN I TELL YOU, HON?

Everyone who met Marion was instantly on first-name terms with her. Several years into our friendship, however, I took to calling her Mrs. Cole in a last-ditch effort to ease some dignity back into her increasingly outrageous life.

My own life had seemed relatively simple at the time we met. I had come to the Hamptons for the summer, not to play, but to finish up some work, and was looking for an unpretentious little house, quiet, inexpensive. By the third day of my search, I was used to the laughter these specifications set off, and was ready to modify them: a room. Anywhere. "You might try Marion Cole down the block," the check-out girl at the supermarket said. "If you're broadminded, that is. Some of her friends are rumored to fly."

It sounded wonderful, and I went to the address at once—a shingled saltbox with a sagging screen door. No one answered the bell, so I poked my head inside. The front room had apparently been abandoned at a moment of cataclysm, like those villas in Pompeii with the table all set, and a knife in the loaf. Here, the artifacts were somehow less poignant. A convertible sofa had not quite made it back together again. A pink plastic curler shared a dish with a quarter pound of soft butter, and Scrabble tiles were scattered over the floor. The only visible movement anywhere was a silently spinning turntable, long since at the end of its tune.

With Marion Cole

The combined smells of Shalimar and cabbage turned me toward the cluttered kitchen, where I glimpsed a woman washing her hair in the sink. Convinced by now that I could do better almost anywhere else, I was tiptoeing away when she straightened up and, pulling aside a swag of dripping hair, peered out at me "Hi, hon!" she cried, as if I'd never been away.

I bumbled out some excuse for being in her house, but she was already busy drying her hair. "Great!" she called through the towel. "Wonderful! Let's get some breakfast going."

It was two in the afternoon, but she quickly scrambled some eggs and found a wedge of banana pie in the fridge. Her friendliness kept suggesting we had already met, but I couldn't recall ever having seen her before. She was not physically memorable, neither young nor handsome. There was no fat on her, but she was solidly made, barefoot in her pink slip, with a round, good-natured face, and lots to say. "Wasn't that a hoot last week?" she cried, winding her damp brown hair around wide rollers. "Phil ought to know better'n to ask Bobby and me to the same bash, because all we do is tango, no matter what the tune."

She rattled on as if, naturally, I knew who and what she was talking about. Edging a word into this wasn't easy, but eventually I made clear I hadn't been at that party. "Well, don't worry, hon, there's another one tomorrow," she said. "If you don't have wheels, I'll borrow Jimmy's old wreck and come get you myself."

I sidestepped this by claiming not to be a party person. "Well, hell, neither am I," she replied. "But—what can I tell you, hon? It's better'n sitting home alone."

We sat at breakfast until dinner time, laughing, talking. I learned she was a widow with two grown sons; but despite a confidential tone, she confided little. It was all small talk. Anything deeper quickly collided with her husky laughter, or one of those nearly meaningless phrases she substituted for opinion. "Oh, *hon*estly!" she would say. Or "Ya dirty rotten kid!" Or "What can I tell you, hon?" Yet in some mysterious way, this starvation fare was nourishing. She was fun. She was warm-hearted. She had, to a remarkable degree, a welcoming presence.

Later that night, we took a tour of the gay discos, and wherever we went, she instantly became the hostess. She called the tune, she set the pace, she hammered out the beat. The Madison was having its brief autocracy, and the dancers, zapped by wildly amplified music, lined up shoulder to shoulder, moving somewhat in unison, like those uncoordinated choruses that were the soul of burlesque shows. I watched and wanted to join in, but only did so when she grabbed my hand and pulled me into the line. "Turn!" she instructed hoarsely. "Again! Left foot! *Left* foot, hon, there you go! Smile, and you can be president!"

It was after four and foggy when I drove her back to her house, neither of us very sober. I'm not sure we had discussed rent, or even the possibility of my living there, but she showed me up to a little slanty-roofed room, and when she had moved the piles of laundry, loose snapshots, and a stuffed pheasant from the bed, she left me to sleep. For better or possibly worse, I had moved in.

Not, I must admit, without second thoughts. When I woke up the next noon, my head was thumping, and the phone downstairs had not stopped ringing. Eventually, I answered it. The caller, asking for Marion, turned out to be someone I knew. "What're you doing at The Madhouse?" he cried. When I told him, he warned, "You won't get a lick of work done there."

"Why not?"

"Wait and see," he said. "*Apres* you, *le deluge*."

I was to find out what he meant that evening. "Quick, they're here!" Marion shouted, as the 7:20 from New York rounded the curve. From her door to the depot was only a minute's run, so we arrived the same moment the train did. "There they are!" Marion cried. "The dirty rotten kids!"

Out of the swarm of weekenders emerged three glowing faces—Jon, Bob, Gary—actually *six* glowing faces, since Jon, Bob, and Gary had each brought a boyfriend. Marion was laughing helplessly as she hugged them. "I don't know where

Marion tricked out for a masquerade.

in hell I'm going to put you all," she admitted.

"But she always manages," Gary told his weekend friend. "Once, she even had 'em sleeping upright in her shower stall."

It didn't quite reach that extreme. Couches were opened up, a spare mattress was unrolled on the floor, one of her guests never returned from the bars that night anyway, and another crawled in with me. Even so, when people began to wake up the next day, the house was densely populated. There was a constant wait to use the bathroom, the telephone, even the narrow stairs. On the other hand, all sorts of invitations began coming in—brunch, cocktails, dinner—so the place was empty most of the weekend after all. The quiet I needed was glorious. I adjusted the lamp in my room, pulled out my typewriter, and got back to work.

It did not occur to me yet that I had come home.

Mondays were always a let-down for Marion. When her playmates returned to the city and secrecy, she seemed left without light. This Monday, however, the darkness was literal. I fussed with the fuse box for twenty minutes before she suggested that maybe the electric bill had not been paid. The unopened mail that had accumulated on and under the table soon verified this; and more. All her utilities, and her town taxes too, were in arrears. "Let's get 'em paid right now," I suggested. "I'll address the envelopes, if you write the checks."

"What checks?" she asked.

I realized suddenly she wasn't kidding. The tact I quickly switched to wasn't necessary, since she was perfectly straightforward about it: somehow, money always got spent before it could be used. All she had coming in was her widow's pension, and the loans her mother occasionally made. "And on Fridays," she added, "I earn a few bucks burning hair." She had set up shop in her kitchen, she explained, and gave shampoos and sets for far less than Mr. Jac at the salon in town. The combs and lotions of her trade were heaped in a frying pan as if waiting for someone to ask for a bacon rinse.

“How about your weekend guests?” I asked. “Don’t they pay you something?”

“My boys?” she cried. “Of course not! They bring their own booze, and—y’know—buy the groceries, and take me out to dinner—“

“They use your house,” I cut in. “They use your hot water and phone. Not to mention your sheets and towels and cologne.”

“I don’t care!” She turned away, stubbornly loyal. “I can’t ask ‘em for money on top of everything else they give me. I may be a slob, but I’m not a whore.”

I paid my next week’s rent early so she could settle the electric bill. The lights blinked back on, but the next week, the phone got shut off, and she came pounding up the stairs to my room. “Can I use your car, hon? It’s urgent!” It had to be, I told her, since her driver’s license had expired. “Then could you drive me?” she begged. “I just got an idea how to shake the money tree.”

We drove a few miles out of town to a cement block dance-bar called the Quarry. It had recently been acquired by Johnny Dio, a tan, unsmiling surfer, but nobody much went there—it was too far out of the way, and when you finally got there, it wasn’t fun. “It’s as simple as this, hon,” she told him, when we arrived. “You got an empty disco, and I got a following—we could make beautiful music together.”

Johnny wanted proof before he committed himself, so that weekend Marion diverted her friends and their friends and *their* friends to the Quarry. The juke box played non-stop, and the cash register made music no less percussive. After that, she was definitely on the payroll, a nightly attraction there, greeting old acquaintance at the door, leading the line dances, and keeping the action fast, sassy, and familial. Nobody in her radius remained a stranger. She seemed never to forget a name. “We’d only met once, and that was five years back,” someone told me, “but when I came into the Quarry, she yelled clear across the room, ‘Why, Gordy Kowdowsky, how *are* you?’”

The change this new job made in her life was immediate. No more fretting about Monday darkness; she kept her lights blazing all the time now. When the Quarry closed for the night, she rushed off with her crowd to someone's house for a drink, a swim, some cards, and the breakfast for fifteen that she somehow invented at daybreak. She'd be getting in about the time I'd be getting up. When I would ask if she'd had fun, her answer was always the same, a phrase I predicted would be carved on her tombstone if she didn't get some rest: "Oh, I had *such* a good time!"

Rest, however, had to share the mornings with her telephone, shower, and the tuna sandwiches she spread up in case anyone got hungry. At noon, five or six of her closest buddies brought her to the beach in her black bathing suit and string of department store pearls. ("You can't beat basic black and pearls," she would say, no matter how often.) As soon as she had spread her towel on the sand, she deserted it to blanket-hop, gadding exuberantly from group to group, playing cut-throat Scrabble, or having a good gossip. She enjoyed hearing all the latest bed news, but I don't recall her speaking unkindly of anyone. Nor did she take sides in the feuds that were the summer's outstanding pastime. Her laughter tended to be raucous, and she could cuss like a roustabout, but she never adopted the boys' jargon, not even words like *gay* and *camp* that even the straight world was starting to use.

On the debit side, she was devoted to dreadful aphorisms, apparently of her own devising. She called her lunch a "tuni-sani", lit up a "smokin' stick", vanished into the dunes to make a "hum-hum," and at the approach of Labor Day, was the hostess of a vast beach "snickeroo." By blackmail or magic, she persuaded Johnny Dio to donate cases of beer, and the supermarket to contribute the hot dogs, while she herself boiled up laundry tubs of night-borrowed corn. There was never enough of anything, which is not surprising since people she had never seen before came out of the surf to enjoy her hospitality. With welcome so general, some of the boys acquired status by not showing up at all.

For not everyone adored her—not even everyone who claimed to. They called her "Mad Marion" and *La Folle*, for she did nothing that she didn't overdo.

If the beach got littered, and the township did nothing about it, she was likely to show up with a stack of plastic trash bags and organize a fete of picking up refuse. And when the commercial fishermen edited their catch and dumped the unsalable sea-robins, skates, and flounders onto the sand, she and her young men would rush up and hurl the flopping, gasping fish back into the ocean. "I got a fellow feeling for 'em," she told me. "Not so long since, I got dumped, myself."

If she never quite explained such statements, others did. Eventually, all of us heard how her father had cut her off. About the disaster of her marriage. About her husband's suicide in the cellar. Not that anyone really believed these stories, but everyone repeated them.

What happened at the posh Estuary Inn was more than hearsay, however. "I was there," the Duke told me much later. "I saw it, I heard it!" Called the Duke of Wellington because of his grand manner, prominent nose, and uncanny resemblance to the Goya portrait, he was literate, well-connected, and—once he had rattled his sabers to establish a defense—kind enough.

"She was there to meet one of the lads for dinner," he confided, "but she was early or he was late, so she was sitting at the bar having a sherry, and even managing to look like quality. And suddenly in swept the deadly Vivian Woodruff and her crowd, high as smoke, my dear, and *livid* because their table wasn't ready. Marion moved a few seats down the bar to make space for them, but either Vivian thought Marion was cutting her, or she couldn't endure a commoner putting her in debt for a courtesy. 'Too kind,' she called to Marion, and turned to her friends. 'I want everyone to meet the Hamptons' most popular fag-hag.'

"Every eye in the place turned to Marion, and the silence, my dear, could have etched glass," the Duke continued. "I mean, Marion would have been justified in hurling her drink in

Vivian's face, but instead, she bowed graciously. 'How do you do,' she called to Vivian's crew. 'Marion Cole, here. Nice to meet you.'

"Such artlessness would have shut up anyone else, but not la Woodruff. She kept trumpeting the same appalling note over and over—fag-hag this, fag-hag that—and each time, Marion somehow harmonized it. When she finally finished her sherry and got up to leave, she even blew a kiss to everyone.

"Of course, I hurried right after her," he added. "She was standing on the porch in a state of shock. 'I didn't know what to say,' she kept bleating. 'What could I say?' I tried to assure her that being gracious had been the perfect rebuke, but she was absolutely sunk." He prolonged a sigh, exaggerated a shrug. "She'd been over-protected by the boys, you see. Because they never catch the irony of her position like another woman does."

"What irony?"

"Oh, you know," he said. "Being female, Marion's the only person in her crowd who never makes out with a guy."

Marion never mentioned the incident to me, yet I wonder now if this humiliation didn't begin to make her good times with the boys an entirely secondary pursuit. Not that it was immediately discernible—-she continued to show up everywhere with a big escort of young men—-yet when I returned to the Hamptons that next spring, it seemed to me she had determined to get a bona-fide man of her own.

"Don't!" she cried, when I started to answer the phone, the night of my arrival. She let it ring several times more, and then, smiling mysteriously, picked up the receiver. "Hello, *you*!" she whispered.

I teased her later. "Got yourself a guy, Mrs. Cole?"

She guffawed. "Millions of 'em!" But her face went red as sunburn.

We never did sit down and talk it out, but the bits and pieces she gradually let fall formed a cohesive mosaic. He was a dentist from Worcester, Jewish, a widower of forty-seven, whom she had been writing to since Lincoln's Birthday. They were not lovers, not yet, but he seemed to be crowding her in that direction. He liked to sing and she liked to sing, he told her, so what was wrong with a duet?

What was wrong was his unexpected arrival at noon, one July day. Marion was at the beach, and I was shaving in her kitchen. I could be explained away, but not that kitchen. Its defiance of three thousand years of sanitary laws sent him running back to his practice in Worcester. Marion was disappointed, but philosophical—attitudes that were promptly swept away by Tom Fletcher.

Fletch was not actually a newcomer in her life. He had gone to high school with her younger sister, but Marion had never paid him any attention. It remained for Gary to do that. "Who's the tall number who just went upstairs?" he whispered.

"Just the mailman," Marion said, not looking up from her jigsaw puzzle. "He stops in to use the toilet."

"He's gorgeous," Gary murmured.

*"Fletch*?" she cried, making two syllables of the name. "That—*gangle*?"

She sneaked a look at him when he came downstairs. Thick black lashes gave his gray eyes a dazzling emphasis, and his body had apparently filled out since the tenth grade. Suddenly, she pushed her puzzle aside. "Anyone here for coffee?" she asked him brightly.

Fletch grinned, his teeth white and even. "No sugar," he said.

He got some, all the same. Every noon, when he dropped by with mail, the coffee was hot, and Marion's hair fluffed out. The piece of toast she began putting by his cup soon became a cookie, and ultimately, a serving of her pound-foolish strawberry shortcake. Then, one night at ten o'clock, I heard a creak on the stairs, and flicked on the hall light. It was Fletch, a little tight. "She here?" he asked sheepishly.

"Still at the Quarry, Fletch."

"Oh," he said. "Well—it's just that I had some letters for her." Self-consciously, he backed down the stairs. "Tell her I'll drop 'em off tomorrow."

She stayed home all the next day, and sure enough, at midnight the mail was delivered. For a week after, I could tell exactly where she was in the house by her singing. He was an ardent lover, but irregular—usually showed up only when he had quarreled with his wife, or had a few drinks in him. "It's like he still stops by just to use the convenience, only now it's me," Marion laughed. None the less, she welcomed him, fed him, arose a half-hour before him at daybreak so he would never see her until she had helped her cause with astringent and cosmetic.

The morning they both overslept added a complexity that this relationship did not need. Marion awoke to find that her mother had dropped by for a shampoo, and was standing at the foot of the bed, eyes wide and mouth narrow.

"Now, Ma," Marion cried. "Damn it, Ma, wait, it doesn't mean a thing!" She rolled out of bed, and hurried down the stairs in pursuit. "Listen to me, Ma! What happened is—see, Fletch is *Gary's* boyfriend. But they quarreled in the middle of the night, so Fletch bunked in with me. Why not? We're like sisters, I couldn't have been safer with a drowned man!"

This explanation stunned Marion's mother into silence, but it had no such effect on Fletch. His virility made suspect, he shouted down the stairs, advising everyone in the house exactly how many times the drowned man had resuscitated during the night, and swearing, by God, never to fucking come back here again. He never did either, unless he was drunk, a condition Marion found less and less acceptable. By the end of August, he was simply sticking her mail through the door-slot in silence, and where he went to the bathroom was anybody's guess.

I had planned to leave the Hamptons after Labor Day, yet I lingered on there. In some crazy way, Marion had provided the family life I was famished for, and I felt unable to leave her until she could regain her composure. It didn't happen overnight. Too often, I would find her sitting in the dark, alone except for a bottle of blend. "It's not that I'm eatin' my heart out for Fletch," she told me. "Maybe I didn't even like him. But I liked—" She fumbled for the word. "—I liked *loving*. I loved having the excuse to care—know what I'm talkin', hon?"

Darkness began to fall earlier. To work off excess energy, I patched the roof, fitted in storm windows, and raked up leaves. When I'd come inside, Marion would have dinner going and a drink waiting. Afterwards, we would play Scrabble, or make hilarious plans for her debut at the Persian Room playing the musical saw. (She actually could.) Gradually, I edged her back into circulation, occasionally trotting her around to the parties she set such store by. It was a healing time for her, but I was increasingly restless.

"Maybe you're working at it too hard," suggested a pleasant guy I met while jogging. "Maybe you need to bust out a bit—sow a few wildflowers, and such."

We did something of the sort. However, Marion, who had never made a fuss about me having overnight guests before, suddenly asked me to cool it—the neighbors were talking, she claimed. Subsequently, when the occasion arose, I simply spent the night out. The icy silences that met me when I returned to her house in the morning apparently didn't warn me enough.

"She's jealous," my new friend told me. "I dropped by to leave you a message today, and, *pow!* she acted like a cast-off wife. Practically tears!"

I had to face her down with it: if she was thinking she and I were seriously playing house, she had better re-think. She tumbled out apologies. "I got my head on wrong, hon," she cried. "It won't happen again, I promise and swear."

But it did. The last time, she made no more promises, and we did not meet each other's eyes. I invented a reason to go to New York the next day, and found other excuses to keep me away. We exchanged postcards and phone calls, but when the next spring came and I returned to the Hamptons, I moved into a place of my own.

My life began to fill out in other directions: new friends,

different pursuits, even an unfamiliar sense of worth. Women's Lib and the Black Revolution had swept into our lives, and now a new wave was racing up the beach—some outraged faggots had dared to resist a police raid in New York, and suddenly a vital young movement was pulling down the figurative stone walls that had for so long segregated us. This change could not last, we warned each other—there was sure to be a violent backlash; yet hope remained white-hot, and Marion was reputed to have raised fifty bucks for the cause by selling paper pansies right under the opposition's nose at a policemen's benefit.

She and I ran into each other occasionally in those years, and always agreeably. We promised to get together soon, but we didn't, and so I know what happened to her mostly by hearsay. It was one of the old ladies she used to curl, for instance, who told me Marion was engaged to be married. "—a responsible man," she confided. "Sixty-ish. Owned a big construction company, but's retired now. And—" She tapped my arm significantly. "—*very* well fixed!"

"How do you know?"

"How, indeed!" she cried. "You should see her engagement ring!"

It was mid-summer before I met him formally—no lesser word could describe the occasion. It was the Historical Society's annual lawn party, and even with the unexpected gusts of wind hitching up long skirts and flapping wide-brimmed hats, it was a more sober affair than those I remembered Marion attending. Yet there she was, strolling up to me, hand outstretched, smiling with new radiance. She was lighter by twenty pounds, and her hair, which had become quite brassy, was now as discreet as chemistry could make it. "I want you to meet Wallace Byrd," she said. "I want you to like him almost as much as I do."

He was a stocky, garrulous man, with wiry gray hair, looking much younger than sixty. He and I chatted agreeably, and Marion backed up his every word with nods and beams. When it came time to part, she once more held out her hand to me, and

I glimpsed the sparkle through her mesh glove. "Show me," I said.

"I was hoping you'd ask," she said, and tugged off the glove. Her hands were always her greatest beauty, and one of the slender tapering fingers set off an exquisite pear-shaped diamond. Even as I exclaimed, the stone slipped around to the side of her finger, as if shy. "Band needs to be smaller," Wallace remarked. "She's dropped so much weight." He winked at her, and I had the impression that, had they been anywhere else, he would have given her a jovial smack on the behind.

She phoned a few days later with an invitation. "Not really a party," she warned. "We're just having a few friends over to see the miracles Wallace hath wrought on this house."

They were extensive. The sagging screen door had been replaced with a gleaming metal one, and it swung open onto a gracious sun-filled room. Upstairs and down smelled of fresh paint and new carpeting. "Everything's in process," Marion laughed. "Every time I get a chance to sit down, the chair's just gone to be re-upholstered. My clothes are all at the seamstress being taken in, my ring's being cut down to size—"

"When's the happy day?"

"Soon as the house is ready."

I told her I knew they'd be happy here, but she shook her head. "We're not planning to live here," she said. "We're only fixing it up so we can sell it. Wallace has a house in Virginia, where he'd like us to live five months a year. Rest of the time, we'll travel." Her eyes sparkled as she told me about it—France in the fall, and during the winter, Switzerland, where they would join the Elliot Roosevelts for skiing. She shook her head, marveling. "*Me*, hon! I just can't believe it."

I couldn't either, although I had no reason not to. Yet I remembered her words a few weeks later, when someone in New York mentioned that Wallace had fled. A bad check had surfaced, and the police came knocking. Even as Marion was coming downstairs to answer the door, Wallace was out the back window and down the alley.

Only then could everyone see how really busy he had been. The diamond ring that had been sent back for sizing was traced to Riverhead where he had pawned it. His home in Virginia, like his big construction company, was a fiction, but his police record in Arkansas was genuine enough. His name turned out not to be Byrd or even Wallace, he had no acquaintance with any known Roosevelt, and, far from being of retirement age, was five years younger than Marion. "He had you all set up," the police chief told her. "Soon as you'd sold your house, he'd have skipped with the cash, and you'd been on the street, crying your eyes out."

Tears were not Marion's usual response to bad luck, however. A week later, she had taken back her old job stirring up fun at the Quarry. Once more, parties became her cure-all, and she rushed from one to another, sometimes four in a night, invited or not, cheerleader at a losing game.

In August, she fainted during a beach picnic. Her sons, serious young men constantly torn between loyalty and mortification, insisted she see a doctor. "I'm fine, I'm fine!" she assured everyone a few days later; but the doctor had laid down some hard-line restrictions. No more booze, for instance. No smoking either, and a rigorous diet. Rest was in, the beach definitely out—walking on sand, he told her, was too much for her heart.

"And if I do all you say," she bargained, "how long will I live? Ten years? Five?"

"Let's put it this way," he replied. "If you don't take it easy—and I mean *easy*—I can't even promise you six months."

She put up with his opinion for a week, but her old enemy, Labor Day, was bringing summer to an end, and the parties marking it were nothing she wanted to hear about second-hand. In the time it took to answer a phone, she was back on the celebration circuit Nor was there any reasoning with her. "What do you want me to do?" she laughed. "Die of boredom?"

She lasted until the new year. The final time I saw her was just after her annual Christmas bash for the boys. Without irony, I asked the old question, "Have any fun?"

Her answer was the same as ever, but her appearance was not. She looked strangely puffy. Or perhaps it was just the way she wore her hair. She had back-brushed it up into a vast blonde pouf, and petrified it with a blast of lacquer which had coincidentally blinded her rhinestone earrings. Her own sparkle persisted, though, and she relayed all the news about people I didn't know, topping it with a familiar challenge: "Want me to beat you at Scrabble?"

I glanced at her daughter-in-law, who was sitting in as nurse. She nodded permission. "You can *try*," I told Marion, "but don't get your hopes up."

Even propped up in bed, she played as she always had, swiftly, and with a passionate conviction that *coq* figured in English usage, and so was permissible in the game. We were nearly through the first set-up, when, inexplicably, she became silent, and her attention contracted inward. The daughter-in-law edged closer. "You okay?" I asked Marion. She nodded, but did not continue playing. I waited uneasily.

"She never had any friends!" she burst out suddenly. "At least I did. I never had anything in my life, *but* friends. And if they were all boys, so much the better."

"Mind telling me what you're raving about?"

"Vivian," she said. "What she called me at the Estuary Inn that night."

I wondered what had sparked this memory, and then noticed I had spelled out the word *hag* on the Scrabble board. "Forget it," I said. "That was ages ago."

She didn't seem to hear. "Sure, I looked after 'em," she defended. "Cooked for 'em, heard their troubles, loved 'em. And they loved me right back, the only relationships I ever had that were worth a hoot in hell! And if that's what she calls being a fag-hag, I don't give a damn!"

I patted her hand, and told her that she had never been a fag-hag. What she was and always would be was an *aide de camp*.

She wasn't listening. Her eyes kept going back to that hateful word on the board, and abruptly she sat up. With sudden resolution, almost as if her next breath depended on it, she planked down her last three tiles, one in front of *hag,* and two after it, transforming it into *shaggy*, a harmless word that ended the game in her favor. She met my eyes with quiet pride. "*Scrabble!*" she said.

## - 14 -

## THE PEARL

Most of the guys I talked to in Union Square had left their fingerprints with the police. But so had I. While my fear of being set up by the cops again had begun to fade, I still could not bring myself to admit to anyone that I had been pulled in on a vag-lewd charge. In some odd way, I found relief in listening to these men who had been through far worse than I, yet seemed able, even eager, to discuss every detail of their sideswipe with the law.

During the hot weather, I usually brought my lunch to the Square. Before long, someone would sit down on the bench beside me and strike up a conversation—could I spare some needful, did I want to buy a Movado watch cheap, was I looking for some fine Columbian leaf? The goods they had for sale weren't anything I was interested in, but the stories they inevitably got around to telling me were.

Georgia Boy, for instance. A big, tawny hustler from Valdosta, he would tell his life story for a "Co-Cola." For two, he'd tell the truth. Both were worth hearing. I was especially impressed by his account of conning five different women in Jacksonville, Florida, into legally adopting him. It impressed the other grifters in the Square too, because soon they were telling the story as if it had happened to *them.*

Over the summer, I got so I could spot such borrowed prestige at fifty paces, and outright lies from half a mile. Not that all the stories I heard were made up. Most of them had at least a grain of truth, but a grain so uncomfortable that the teller had coated it over and over with soft soap so he could live with it—sort of like what an oyster does in the formation of a pearl. However, true or false, I wrote each of their stories down in my notebook when I got home.

Eventually these began to fuse together in a wide pattern, and characters started moving around in it. The most special of these was a big child-like illiterate I called Babe. As his adventures gradually unfolded in my imagination, I started to shadow after him in fact—in the interest of accuracy, began doing on-the-spot research at his hangouts—the train yards, the hobo jungles, the small-town jails. What slowed down this investigation, however, were the big slammers. While I managed to land a job as a guard in a prison road camp outside Oviedo, Florida, I couldn't get inside the major penitentiaries. It is ironic that after all my nightmare efforts to keep out of prison, I was now struggling to bust in, and being turned away.

*So the door's locked, you crawl in a window,* is old housebreaker logic. Since lack of education is such a conspicuous cause of crime, and I was more or less qualified to instruct, I figured a volunteer teacher in the rehabilitation program for convicts would always be welcome. However, I found out that in the fifty-mile radius of my doorstep, no such educational plan was being offered in prisons. "Unless you'd want to teach Sunday school," said the Lieutenant at a big institution on Long Island. He was a heavy-set man with a face as flat as a thumb print. "There's always an opening for someone who knows the Bible."

I had only the slightest background in the Gospel, but claimed to be an authority. "You'll need to be," the Lieutenant told me. "We got boys here who really know their Bible. You hear 'em quarreling sometimes, not shouting obscenities at each other, but curses from the Old Testament by chapter and verse. '*Genesis four-eleven to you!*' one of 'em screams at some enemy down the corridor. 'Yeah?' the other yells back. '*Well,*

*Deuteronomy twenty eight- seventeen right back at you!'"*

My palms got wet, waiting for the Lieutenant to ask if I'd ever been arrested —if that secret were discovered, I'd be kicked out at once. No such question was ever asked, however, and the next Monday, I was allowed to pass behind the high penitentiary walls and join the other Sunday school teachers: two women and a Mr. Wilton. The little cement block chapel on the third floor was bleak, but clean, and one of the ladies put a few sprigs of honeysuckle in a pleated paper cup. Around six o'clock, our convict congregation began straggling in, mostly young, and predominantly black. A guard sat at the rear, armed and ready in case opinions differed. Our staff read aloud from the Bible, after which, we sat down with the boys in small groups, and for the rest of the hour discussed their personal problems in light of the Scripture. There was no collection, and no music, although once, the older of our two ladies sang *Lead, Kindly Light* in an inadvertently bluesy voice. "'Make a joyful noise unto the Lord,'" Mr. Wilton quoted, with approval.

Nearly every occurrence inspired Mr. Wilton with an appropriate quotation. This amused me at first, but then, one night after class, he turned it on me. As I shook his hand before parting, he peered into my face and lowered his voice. "'Thou shalt not bear false witness" he rebuked.

"What do you mean?" I demanded.

"You're not here to spread the Word, are you?" he accused. "You're here for some peculiar reason of your own." His eyes searched me. "Some kind of newspaper reporter, perhaps? Looking for an inside scoop?"

"*Me?* Don't be funny!"

"I've seen you taking notes," he persisted.

I gave the careless shrug I had learned from the inmates, but the threat of exposure alarmed me. "Are you going to tell the Lieutenant?" I asked.

"I'll have to think about it," he said. "I'll give it some prayer."

From then on, I watched him uneasily, waiting for him to

inform on me. Balding, and beginning to put on weight, Wilton was an automobile salesman whose special gift was reaching prodigals, and directing them home to a loving Father. For all his platitudes, he became absolutely direct when he sat down with the young convicts, most of whom had grown up without any mature male influence. Some responded at once to his urgency, but when all else failed, he would heap sympathy on their loneliness until they broke down. It seemed a kind of emotional rape to me, and yet by the time he lent them his handkerchief, he usually had them ready to change their ways. LeeRoy, the most unruly of our regulars, had not been put in isolation since Mr. Wilton had shaken him up. Neither had Junior or Highpockets. Only Donnie stayed cheerfully unaffected.

Donnie never seemed to get the idea he had done anything that needed correction. He was like a puppy who bounds about playfully when menaced with the slipper he has just chewed up. Tall and good-looking, this engaging young Black was perfectly ready to oblige whoever had his ear, whether it was Mr. Wilton or the neighborhood drug lord. "I don't think you're taking correction seriously," the judge had told him, when Donnie was arrested for pushing dope a week after serving a year for the same offense. "I'm going to see that you stay off the streets until you can live by the rules."

Mr. Wilton asked Donnie if he knew what rules were, and Donnie said he did. "But after he'd been explaining for a minute," Wilton told me, "I realized he was talking about playing basketball."

Reclaiming Donnie was soon his primary focus. "That boy doesn't realize he has any worth," he kept telling the ladies. In an effort to give Donnie some sense of his own value, Wilton piled on the praise whenever the young man remembered to say "thank you"; lauded him for not whispering to the others during silent prayer, and even commended him publicly for using a handkerchief.

Still, there wasn't much time left to change him. The prison only held a convict until he could be processed to a larger penitentiary such as Sing Sing or Auburn, and Donnie's transfer was imminent. Mr Wilton tripled his efforts, but nothing seemed to sink in until their final meeting, when the two were saying goodbye. "So, hey, take care yourself, man," Donnie told Mr. Wilton. He slapped the older man's palm, basketball style. "See you aroun', okay?"

Mr. Wilton caught his hand, and holding it between both of his, met Donnie's eyes squarely. "Go with God, Donnie," he said. "He loves you, and so do I."

Donnie started to grin, and then didn't. Something apparently happened in him that his face wasn't used to. The other cons, shoving out of the chapel, swept him along, but the look he turned back was of such sudden illumination that the lady with the bluesy voice whispered, "*Bingo!*"

During the week, Wilton phoned me at home. He had just received a letter from Sing Sing, and with a voice full of glory, announced that Donnie had unequivocally decided to follow the Better Path. "He says it's something he's never tried before, but that nothing else in his life had paid off, so why not give it a go?" Wilton's spirits soared as he quoted a citation about the joy in heaven over one sinner saved.

I said I was glad to hear this, but in fact, I was pestered by quite another feeling. It seemed to me that neither man had remotely understood the other's message. Some irreverent sense kept suggesting that Donnie had put a strictly jailhouse spin on Mr. Wilton's statement that he loved him. In which case, Donnie's willingness to "give it a go" might not be quite what Wilton had in mind.

The collision with reality had already begun when I arrived at the chapel the following Monday. Wilton's greeting seemed distracted. At the first opportunity, he slipped me a letter that had apparently arrived that day. "*Read this!*"

Donnie's handwriting was hard to make out. Here and there, I could decipher some really awful endearments, but only his request for a new pair of high-priced Nike sneakers was entirely legible. The signature, however, was blurred by the imprint of a kiss.

Wilton appeared to have recovered somewhat by the end of prayer meeting, but two days later, he telephoned me in whispered despair. "Oh, God," he said. "Donnie's sent me a tracing of his member."

He had already decided to stop writing any more letters to the young convict. This, however, did not stop Donnie from writing to him. Another letter came a few days later, reminding Wilton about the new sneakers, and visualizing the day when he would be free, and they could move in together. "Man," Donnie promised, "we sure gone melt down that ol' bed."

Reason was no comfort to Mr. Wilton this time. I told him that Donnie would probably have forgotten this romantic intention by the time he had served his sentence. "After all, he's still got a couple of years to go."

"We don't know that," Wilton cried. "They're letting prisoners out earlier every year now. And he knows where I live, I gave him my address so he could write to me. By summer, he could be standing on my doorstep with his suit-case, ready for I don't know what. Can you imagine how I'll explain to my wife?"

He began pacing back and forth. "Oh, Lord," he groaned, "I don't know what to do."

"I know what *I'd* do," I said.

I told him, but he rejected the suggestion unconditionally. "That would break about half the Commandments in the Decalogue," he protested. "Just what I'd expect of you!"

However, another letter from Sing Sing apparently arrived soon after—one especially fraught with erotic enthusiasm, I suspect, because the next week, Wilton was waiting for me in the prison parking lot, so agitated that he scarcely gave me time to get out of my car. "All right then, have it your way," he cried. "Only it'll have to be in your handwriting, because he'd recognize mine."

He had the note paper ready, and told me what to put down. "Dear Donnie," he dictated, "it is my sad duty to inform you that dear Mr. Wilton died in his sleep last night—"

It was a long letter full of reverence for the deceased, and he had me sign it "Mary Burns, registered nurse." Once this was mailed, we heard no more from Donnie.

But it was not the last I heard about the episode. Every time I met Wilton at Sunday school, he had a new explanation for it. These grew to be more and more removed from the original incident, increasingly aglow with nobility and sacrifice, and culminating, he claimed, in Donnie's permanent redemption. By the end of the year, Wilton had turned his little grain of truth into a really spectacular pearl.

I never let on about this to the Lieutenant, of course. And you can be sure Wilton never let on about me.

Agnes de Mille

# - 15 -

## EATEN ALIVE

She came into the University Place coffee shop for breakfast every morning. The imperious nose and raveled-rope hair easily identified her as Agnes de Mille, but the customers were New Yorkers, used to celebrities, and gave no sign that they noticed. The counter man, however, served her cautiously. "Don't get in her way, buddy," he told me once. "She'll eat you alive."

I didn't doubt him for a moment. Ever since she had burst into the public awareness with her stunning choreography for *Oklahoma!* some twenty years before, she had earned a reputation for fierce independence. I watched her carefully as she ate her scrambled eggs each day, hoping she would do something characteristic that would make a good letter home. She spoke to no one, however, and seldom looked up from the book she brought along, or the manuscript she was correcting. But then, one February morning, she upset her coffee cup.

Leaping up, she snatched her papers out of harm's way, spattering droplets onto the suddenly hunched shoulders of other customers. As the counter man stayed well out of it, I grabbed some paper napkins and tried to blot up the mess. Perhaps she suddenly realized everyone was watching, possibly enjoying, for she tossed her head, and, gathering up her purse and papers, stalked out of the coffee shop. The counter man leaned forward. "See what I'm sayin'?" he said. "She's probably blamin' you for it already."

That possibility seemed even more likely when she marched up to me the next morning. "Are you the young man of yesterday?" she demanded. I nodded, and braced myself for her reprimand. Instead she thanked me briskly, and opened her purse. I had a sudden fear she was going to give me a quarter, and said, "No, no, it was my pleasure." Except what I said was "my pressure." And anyway, she was only taking her glasses out of her purse. She searched my face for some sign of coherence, then once more marched away.

Yet after that she sometimes nodded to me. Once she remarked that it was a dreadful morning; once observed that spring had finally arrived. It seemed too tenuous a connection to survive the two weeks I had to be out of town, however, and on my return, I passed her at the counter without making any effort to renew our acquaintance. While she clearly did not like to be bothered, neither apparently would she tolerate being ignored, and on her way out, she addressed me. "You've been away." She meant it kindly, I expect, but it sounded like an accusation.

I told her I had been in Philadelphia. That could mean only one thing to her. "With the try-out of that new musical?" she asked. Even before I admitted it, she took stock of my lanky frame. "But surely you're not a dancer!"

I explained I was a writer called in to help with revisions. She examined my answer thoughtfully, then sat down beside me and asked about my work—wanted to know if I had ever had anything produced or published, and who I liked to read. She too wrote, she admitted.

I had, in fact, read two of her books, and was able to come up with the title of one, the autobiographical *Dance to the Piper*. Her eyes were direct, but seemed neither pleased nor surprised at anything I said. Yet when she stood up, it was as if I had passed some kind of test. "All right," she said, "come have a drink with me at five tonight."

To make clear that I was accepting an invitation and not obeying a command, I arrived a little late. I had been told to ask the elevator man for "Mrs. Prude," and he took me up to the ninth floor. A plump French housekeeper ushered me into the living room. Still lit by sunset, it was handsome and comfortable, full of things that were meant to be discovered. A shelf of bound theatre magazines from turn-of-the-century Paris looked especially tempting. Above the fireplace was a portrait of de Mille that seemed to be made of those bright candy dots and dashes that sprinkle children's birthday cakes. I saw fine Meissen figurines, a flat basket of annotated musical scores, and some of the awards she had won for great Broadway musicals. *Brigadoon. Carousel.* A bronze bronco commemorated her ballet, *Rodeo.* I could have browsed happily for several hours, but her brisk footstep in the hall announced that she, at least, kept no one waiting.

She served me a glass of sherry, but was so impatient to discuss what was on her mind that small-talk became microscopic. Suddenly, she pushed a sheaf of papers toward me. "Read this!"

I was aware of her watching intently as I read, which only added to the strain. This was the opening chapter to another book of memoirs, but unlike *Dance to the Piper,* this seemed to be cover-to-cover complaint. It was not just the raw anger of a woman having to compete in a field that had always been dominated by men, she also worked in the long-time feud with her powerful uncle, Cecil B. De Mille, and trashed heredity for giving her a body so unsuitable for a dancer. I began to feel besieged, and she sensed it immediately. "You don't much care for the book, do you?" she said. "The fact is, you dislike it intensely." When I tried to answer with tact, she interrupted. "Nothing but utter frankness can possibly help me."

We talked about her chapter for nearly an hour, but "utter frankness" seemed to antagonize her as much as diplomacy. When I left, it was with the feeling that I had lost any chance of ever getting to look at her volumes of *fin de siecle* theatre.

Yet when she came into the coffee shop, the following day, she sat down beside me. "I expect I was very rude last night," she said. "At all events, it wasn't you I was impatient with, it was myself, my own limitations."

She ordered coffee for us both, and, stirring more than she sipped, spoke passionately of what was waiting to be achieved in the theatre, in literature and dance. It was a magnificent vision, one that she was to call to my attention again and again, over the years. She was helplessly a teacher, and even as we sat there at the counter, I had a vision too: that of a tigress licking a cub into shape.

Only as we parted that morning, did she mention her memoirs again. "I've put that chapter aside until it calms down," she said briskly. "You have to let creative work develop in tranquility."

*Tranquility* was the no-win word. I saw precious little of it in her, then or ever. Controversy seemed to be her natural element. Even when we would appear to agree, I would suddenly discover we were on opposite sides. Neither of us, for instance, had a good word to say for censorship. How was it, then, that after a lively discussion of it, we stopped speaking for two weeks?

"And if you think that was bad," said one of her former friends, with a sharp smile, "wait till she finds out that you're gay."

"I'm sure she must know already," I said.

"Then she's saving it to finish you off with." The smile grew sharper. "Wait!"

The sort of stress she subjected her friendships to only hinted at the pressure she put on herself. Most of her creative work seemed to be done under the most harrowing tension. Backstage or in shabby rehearsal halls, hounded by traffic noises, arguments in the wings, and an ever-nearing opening date, she could be seen straining to transform some elusive emotion into a complex pattern of movement. When inspiration faltered, her dancers would stand waiting while she paced back and forth, her clasped hands pressed to her brow, every tendon tightened in an effort to force out some innovation. Little wonder, her dancers slyly pronounced her first name "Agonize."

Yet it was at rehearsal that one could most nearly come to know this driving and driven woman. I think immediately of a winter day in a West Fifty-Seventh Street studio when *The Four*

*Marys* was taking shape. Structurally, the ballet was nearly complete, but the rich characterizations, always the heart of a de Mille work, were still unrealized by the dancers. Persistently, even with patience, de Mille kept clarifying the emotional relationships, inventing the revealing gesture, improving, refining, encouraging. When a principal ballerina seemed unable to project a certain quality, Agnes took over the role herself to illustrate what she wanted. Lightly touching her partner's arm, this middle-aged woman in mud-spattered galoshes moved forward to the music, seamlessly transfigured into a tender, trusting girl, glowing with beauty. It wasn't mere performance. The beauty was de Mille's own, but I had never seen it before. The costume designer standing beside me had the explanation. "It's hard for her to let go in real life," he said. "You come to realize she's only herself when she can be someone else."

Generally, she was too busy to make the most of how she looked. Too busy, or too self-conscious. "My sister inherited Mother's beauty," she said once. "I got Father's nose." She made a magnificent appearance on first nights and for curtain calls, but on ordinary occasions, seemed satisfied if one shoe matched the other. When a tour took her to Moscow, she told one of her dancers, "I must be looking particularly dowdy today—everybody keeps coming up to me and speaking Russian."

Paradoxically, her increasing fame had begun to limit her opportunities on Broadway—few directors wanted to share authority with her, and opted instead for a choreographer less likely to take over. Consequently, Agnes began focusing her fierce energies elsewhere, forming her own dance company, hustling for its endowment, creating its ballets, and endlessly drawing the public's attention to it with her appearances on television. This last, though it was great for business, seemed a terrible trial to her. "Too competitive," she said.

What she meant by this, I didn't learn until the September day her son left home to enter college. "—and as if that wasn't enough to bear," she said on the telephone, "I have to watch myself on TV in a few minutes. Could you come over and be moral support?"

The uncertainty in her voice was too rare to ignore, and I hurried down the block to her address. The windowless room I was shown into contained little beside the television set and two rocking chairs. Agnes was hunched down in one of these, looking like an old-maid schoolmarm: her mouth was bleak, her dress wrinkled, and her graying hair skewered back. In contrast, the TV screen was beginning to show a stately image moving down a long corridor to sonic booms of Russian music. It was herself in a velvet ball gown that showed off her beautiful bosom and her mother's jewels. Drawing in close to the camera, she threw her head back and graciously announced, "I am Agnes de Mille." The woman in the rocking chair sat up contentiously. "The hell you are, honey," she growled.

Although her dances are full of delicious insights, and she often spoke with great wit, I have never been certain she had a sense of humor. Yet sometimes, especially during the summer, she lapsed unaware into fun. "Come out to Merriewold for the weekend," she would call up and say. "We'll be very informal, just family."

Family was her husband, Walter Prude, a well-made, crisply assured man, and their son, Jonathan, then in his teens. The estate had been her playwright father's, and was several hours' drive from the city, an unpretentious farmhouse in the Catskills. There was a lake nearby, and acres of woods, where dappled shadows sometimes turned out to be deer. Nothing much was ever planned. We wandered, we ate, we read. A volume pulled from the shelves was likely to have John Barrymore's bookplate in it, or an affectionate inscription from Mary Martin. Agnes seemed almost relaxed here—even on the day Paulette, her French housekeeper, overturned the table of priceless Canton china. The whole household sat out in the sunshine, casually gluing it back together. Conversation, when it happened at all, was lazy and frequently backward in glance.

"I never knew Joan Crawford well, when I was a girl in Hollywood," Agnes mused. "My mother and father didn't approve of her—Joan was a starlet in those days, and you know what *that* meant! But when I was raising money for the ballet company recently, I wrote her a note, reminding her that we had been girls together, and she phoned up the next day inviting me to drop by—"

She seemed to relish each detail of Crawford's huge two-story apartment in New York. "—clear plastic slip-covers over everything, my dear, like a provincial bordello—" "—couldn't see a toilet anywhere in her bathroom, until it occurred to me that that ruffled hoopskirt in the corner might be—" "—and her bedroom! Oh, God, it was incredible! So bloody pink! Not an ordinary baby pink," she added. "Not rose pink either, but the color of—" She searched the distances for the exact shade she had in mind. "—the color," she said suddenly, "of cheap dentures!"

My favorite evening there occurred when Jan Peerce, the grand old tenor of the Metropolitan Opera, phoned to remind Agnes that she and her party were coming to his opening at some big Catskill hotel that night. "I'd forgotten all about it," she confessed when she hung up. "Really hate to disappoint him—but—"

I understood her hesitation: these openings were ritually gala, and the clothes I had brought along were scarcely fit for a picnic. I urged the rest of them to go without me, but that was too much like surrender for Agnes. "We'll *all* go, or none!" she stated. "My God, what am I known for, if not pulling rabbits out of hats?"

The attic yielded up a dinner jacket from her late father's wardrobe. It fitted me in only three places, but Agnes let down the sleeves as far as possible. As moths had made off with the trousers, Walter volunteered some navy blue slacks. They were too large, but "you'll be sitting down most of the time anyway." I borrowed a dress shirt and tie from Jonathan, which left only shoes to be extemporized, and we finally dyed a pair of maroon leather bedroom slippers with India ink. Nobody suggested that the conglomerate look would revolutionize men's wear, but I had a wonderful time. Peerce was magnificent, the crowd was jeweled and jubilant, and by the next week, the India ink had finally worn off my feet.

Yet even the relaxed atmosphere of Merriewold could not exorcize Agnes for long. The memory of some injustice would suddenly spur her into recrimination, a savage eloquence that was exhausting to her, and a strain on the listener.

Once this began, she would end a friendship before she would change the subject. It was she, one realized, who was eaten alive.

Typical was the anger she directed at Richard Rodgers and Oscar Hammerstein II. "Did I or did I not make a notable contribution to those shows?" she would demand. "It made them millions in royalties. Millions! And what do they toss me in appreciation? Loose change! Nickels and dimes, so that I have to scramble around and beg people for enough money to keep my dancers alive."

Eventually, I asked her if she wasn't afraid such recurrent anger would finally destroy the lyric quality that was her greatest gift. She tossed her head. "For all you know," she retorted, "that anger *is* my lyric quality."

They lived side by side in her, the madrigal and the jeremiad, the voluptuous and the chaste. She was often in love, and yet as far as I know, never strayed outside her marriage. This delicate balance was unconsciously achieved by falling in love only with young men who could not quite reciprocate. Her romance with a handsome, but totally paralyzed English boy is legend today. So were her infatuations with male dancers, good looking and intelligent, but gay.

Ironically, she was very antagonistic to homosexuality, and I found her constantly trying to find out which side I stood on. In an effort to preserve our friendship, I became increasingly guarded. This, however, offended her almost as much as an open admission—the very act of holding something back seemed either perverse or unnatural. I barely escaped with my life, one night, when I took her to a play of mine off-Broadway, *Shout from the Rooftops*. After the final curtain, while we were trying to hail a cab, I asked her how she had liked it. According to my journal, her answer was succinct: she didn't.

I laughed. "Love your tact, dear."

"Tact is your strategy, not mine," she retorted. "Read my books, hear me lecture, then ask what I spare even myself. Do I try to pass myself off as sweet-tempered, gentle, or even gentile? Do I hide my failures, my pressure, my impossible drive? No! Every wart is there to be seen, every card face-up on the table. Can you say the same?"

I was silent, and she moved closer, her voice passionate and persuasive. "Caution, diplomacy, tact—they have no place in creative people. A writer should *use* his fear instead of hiding it. He should make everything work for him, bring it all out in the open—anger, failure, shame! All of it!"

I knew what she was addressing, and for an instant was tempted to own up about myself. However, my arrest had made me distrustful of straight people—they had used my honesty as a weapon against me before, and I was not about to repeat that mistake. Instead, I stepped out into the street, and shouted at a passing car, "*Cab!*" Being a private vehicle, it did not stop, but the suddenness and stridency of my voice broke the tension and successfully changed the subject.

However, she always brought it back, and our rapport began to suffer. Suddenly it fell apart. One day, I mentioned one of her dancers, the beautiful Betty Low, for so many years my closest friend, and abruptly Agnes wheeled on me. "Why did you never marry her?" she demanded. "Why have you never married at all?"

"My God," I cried, " you'd think you and I were married, the nagging I put up with."

My voice was too loud, my face too close. She drew herself up with towering dignity, and as she turned away, blindly

Betty Low in Agnes de Mille's *Bloomer Girl.*

plowed into a little table, knocking it over. That did it! My reply she could dismiss or even top, but no one saw her make an awkward move, and lived.

Our reconciliation was not easy. That same year, I began spending more and more time on the east end of Long Island. Occasionally, I wrote Agnes a note, and occasionally received a reply. She sent me some tickets to a gala concert in which she was to appear in the City, but our plans changed suddenly with the news that she had had a stroke. I drove to the hospital at once, bringing some lilies from my garden. I was not allowed to see her, of course, nor were the people who knew her far better than I. She was alive, but the word in the corridors was that death would be kinder for someone who lived so intensely for the nuance of movement.

Yet Agnes would not be written off so easily. I followed the progress of her recovery, although it was a long time before our actual communication resumed. Once in a while, we spoke on the phone. Each time, the slur in her speech was less noticeable; but healing was slow. It was not for another two years that I actually saw her again.

She had invited me to lunch. Her apartment, at least, was the same as ever. Waiting for her to be brought in, I traced my fingertips along the row of bound theatre magazines I had never had time to open. The little porcelain Bacchus I had once mended was still on a shelf. Then I heard her call from an inner room, peremptorily advising her luncheon guests, "Don't anyone help me!"

In she came, clad in a great coral-colored caftan, pushing a light metal walker in front of her. It was indeed Agnes, damaged but indomitable, a perambulating sibyl, carefully made up as if for the stage, her thinned white hair drawn back by a green chiffon bow. As she made the round of her guests, her glance was keen, and she was cordial, but she did not smile. The hand she held out to me seemed boneless, the consistency of a breast.

Speaking as precisely as ever, and as unceremoniously, she led the way to the table. No one was allowed to do anything for her. Although her food had been prepared so she could eat it with minimal effort, she still favored her left hand. As always, she dominated the conversation, and only once seemed at a loss for words. This happened when I passed around an old snapshot I had found in a Kensington curio shop. It was of Agnes in Algerian costume, taken when she was a young dancer struggling to make her name in London. She examined the photograph searchingly, so silent that others at the table became silent too, and I thought I had made a mistake in bringing it. "Yes," she said with sudden vigor. "The Bazaar Girl. She was one of my best—a characterization I did at concerts and private parties, back then. Not really a dance at all—it was acting too, and singing."

"You *sang*?" someone asked.

To prove it, she raised her voice in a loud, completely unmodulated Algerian street song, as much a come-on as a lament. There was nothing here of de Mille, the self-guarded monument. Sitting at the head of the table was an unwashed Moorish baggage, clinking with bangles, her bold kohl-encircled eyes punctuating her song with quick, hard glances at the passersby. Even when the wail of her words ended, she loudly hummed her own accompaniment, and, never moving from her chair, delivered the requisite undulations. Chewing betel nuts, sometimes spitting, her eyes half-closed, she wove her arms about, serpent like, and by pressing her palms together above her brow, formed the outline of a mosque dome, in which her head smoothly slid from side to side. I suddenly realized that, deeply absorbed in her characterization of the girl, Agnes was unconsciously using muscles the doctor had pronounced dead. She realized this at the same moment, and our eyes met in astonishment.

I winked at her, but this moment was too special for her to share with anyone. She turned her head toward the housekeeper, once more rigidly inaccessible. "I think you might bring in the dessert now," she said.

## - 16 -

### *A CREDIT TO SOCIETY*

My younger sister, Noo, cried at the wedding. She didn't know the bride very well, but the groom and most of the guests at the reception had been her friends at school, and she seemed determined to introduce me to each one of them. Their names had all begun to sound alike by the time she presented me to a solemn man in a morning coat. *Dexter* was all I heard, and it seemed to echo.

"Who was *that?*" I whispered, as we walked away.

"Father of the bride," Noo said. "Why?"

"No reason," I said. Yet a moment later, I had to ask, "Is Dexter his first name, or last?"

"First," she said. "Is he someone you've met before?"

"I'm not sure," I told her. "I think when I was little, he lived at the end of our block."

"Want to go back and ask him?"

Wanted to, yes. Just the same, I didn't. If he was who I thought, what could I say to him? You can't just go up to a man at his daughter's wedding reception, and ask, "Was it you who sexually molested me when I was five?"

I was too savvy to believe that, except for him, I might have grown up straight—after all, his delinquency had apparently not altered *his* genetic direction —yet the impulse to kid him about it persisted. All the next day, I entertained myself by picturing his reaction to my blockbuster question. Sometimes he backed away in confusion, sometimes his nostrils flared dangerously, and he ordered me out of the place. In my more realistic fantasies, he looked at me vacantly, without the faintest idea of what I was talking about. The fact was, I had only a foggy recollection of what had happened, myself. Parts of the image would start to take shape—the sullen expression of his eyes, for instance—and then fade out just an instant short of certainty.

There had been a lot of half-remembering since I had returned to Los Angeles after so many years—a constant and thwarting sense of *déjà vu:* faces I almost remembered, names I nearly recalled, streets that were familiar, yet led nowhere. Even when my hunches turned out to be right, time had already cancelled them. The day we drove along Santa Monica Beach, for instance. "Am I crazy?" I asked Noo. "Didn't there used to be a big sugar loaf of a rock here? We called it Charlie Chaplin's Rock, or something."

She nodded. "Castle Rock, really. Only it was declared unsafe a few years ago, and they dynamited it."

Actual confrontation with the past exploded things just as effectively. One afternoon, I happened past the grammar school where my older sister Sharlie had gone to first grade, and it was not at all the intimidating brick fortress I remembered, but small and rather faded, with paper cut-outs pasted on the windows. And on the day after the wedding reception, when I obeyed an impulse to find the house my family had rented during my early years, I couldn't even recall how to get there. Yet surely, I reasoned, if I had sat beside my mother as she drove home from market every day, long ago, the directions must still be in my head. Putting myself in neutral, I just kept driving about, susceptible to any hint, waiting to be shown. Suddenly making an unexpected turn, I found myself looking down a street I didn't instantly recognize, but which identified itself by the rush of sensation up my spine.

This quickly changed to disappointment. Only the street sign was the same.

I remembered the number of our house—3944—but the building at that address was now a top-heavy modern duplex whose upstairs windows flaunted orange curtains that would have made Bauma, my mother's mother, roll her expressive eyes to heaven. The oaks that lined the boulevard were still there, but the monumental peach tree I used to climb was gone, and the Saturday smell of backyard incinerators had long since been outlawed. The entire frame of reference of my early childhood was suddenly threatened, and in an effort to re-establish it, I parked the car and walked up the block, peering about for substantiation. Brown iris still grew in our neighbor's yard, though I had not recalled them as being so ugly. The dark, genteel residence where The Society Lady (as we used to call her) had lived was still standing, but was weathered now, with a For Sale sign stuck in the lawn. The final house on the block was white instead of the gray it once was, and the two-car garage behind it had been rebuilt. A curious clash of childish alarm and curiosity authenticated the site: this is where Dexter had lived. Suddenly, his last name flashed through me. Hasbrook. Dexter Hasbrook.

The other facts did not shoot into place so spontaneously. While the general picture swept over me now like a silent avalanche, most of the details only sneaked back when I was thinking of something else the following week—lying on the beach, having lunch alone at the Farmers' Market, waiting in some agent's outer office. Nothing was in chronological order, and much of it was wildly irrelevant. An earlier cadence began to fill my ears, and all of it, even the most inconsequential, still seemed charged with the excitement of a five-year-old boy knowing something that the grown-ups didn't.

This secret had been so big, I was scarcely able to move without spilling it. Trouble was, none of my family was around to spill it to. My sister Sharlie had abandoned me for the first grade. My dad left for his office in downtown Los Angeles right after breakfast every day, and my mother rested a lot—she was making a nest under her heart, Bauma said. Even Bauma herself was too busy to listen to me, this being her day to make gingersnaps. I hopped around the kitchen on one foot, getting in her way until she had to notice. "What is it, Buddy?"

I tried to tell her what had happened, but now that I had her attention, I couldn't find any of the words I needed. Usually I had no trouble telling anyone anything. My dad said I was the all-time standing-up sitting-down champion talker. He called me J. Bud Jabberjaw because I had so much to tell. Like the day I found the dead gopher. Or the time I was brushing my teeth in front of the mirror, and suddenly realized I was alive. That had been hard to explain, but not so hard as this. So I kept talking about everything else first—my cousin Billly's visit, and the tree house I wanted to build. Finally I managed to tell her about wandering down the block and climbing up the barrels in Dexter Hasbrook's garage. Except the new batch of gingersnaps was ready to take out of the oven just then, and Bauma turned back to it. She gave me a cookie still hot, and told me to run along and play.

So I went upstairs. I nearly always did what she wanted, because she was my favorite person. Or anyway, next to my mother, she was. Her eyes were bright, and she was soft to sit on. She wanted me to grow up to be a credit to society, and an architect. Bauma was more fun than my other grandmother, and wore a long string of amber beads that she said were tears a tree had wept for her. Another reason I liked her was the look on her face when she'd ask which hand do you want. Even better was the way she sang the song about the girl who hid in a chest on her wedding day, and wasn't found till she was moldering bones. Bauma was a natural-born actress, my father said. He liked to tease her by saying terrible things so she would react. When I was born, he told her I looked like a baked potato. She drew the air up her nose, and said, "Why, that's a *beautiful* baby!" My dad said the look on her face was a doozer! It was a word he said a lot, but Bauma didn't like me to use it. She said it was slang, and gentlemen didn't.

What gentlemen did was very important to Bauma. Gentlemen kept their hands clean all the time, and told the truth, and wore their garters. My cousin Billy didn't have to wear garters, and called me a sissy. I didn't like him much. We had a cedar chest in our hall, but I couldn't think of any way to make him get into it and molder. Anyway, I cut those old garterrs with Bauma's fingernail scissors, and told her they had fallen apart.

She didn't believe me. She found the garters in the wastebasket, and told me they had not fallen apart at all, but had been *cut.* I could not understand how she had figured that out so easily. I began to wonder if she knew everything else I hadn't told her. I wondered especially if she knew what had happened in the garage up the block.

In case she already knew, I said, "I went into Dexter Hasbrook's garage." She said "Oh?" and asked if Dexter Hasbrook was someone I played with. I said yes, But I did not say that Dexter Hasbrook was grown up.

He wore long trousers and slicked his hair straight back, and went to junior high. He did not get mad when he found me playing in his garage, but he did not smile. I had never talked to grown boys before. Or rather, they had never talked to me. Except Dexter Hasbrook didn't really talk, he just whispered, and looked back over his shoulder. He took out his thing, and wanted to put it in my mouth. I didn't want to. So he sat down on a box, and pulled me onto his lap. He opened my pants and rubbed my thing with his handkerchief. It did not hurt, but after a while I got tired of it, and went home.

I forgot all about him after Jonie moved next door to our house. She was from Seattle, the same age as me, five going on six, with yellow hair cut in bangs. "Blonde, blonde, as a willow wand," Bauma sang. I do not know why she liked Jonie, because she used slang all the time, and was sassy. Her mother and father were divorced. She had a big box of crayons, and when we played together, she drew red crayola on her lips.

We found some shelf paper in my room, and cut out a lady twice as tall as we were. Then we scribbled her face pink, and her dress blue and orange, and Jonie told me about the boys in Seattle peeing up against trees. We started talking about it, and then, somehow, we got on the bed and took our clothes off.

I had nearly always known how different little boys were from little girls, but it had never occurred to me before that, the way she went in and the way I stuck out, we could fit together like a jigsaw puzzle. When we mashed them together, they sort of did. Except this is when Bauma opened the bedroom door and looked in.

Jonie tried to hide behind the pillow, and I did too, but I could see the expression on Bauma's face. It was a doozer. She ordered Jonie to put on her clothes and go home at once. I got very upset when she said she would have to tell my mother. I told her if she did, I wouldn't be an architect, I'd be a burglar. She said she didn't much care what I did now, and that made me so mad, I reached up and gave her string of amber beads a yank. They went bouncing all over the floor. I don't remember if we picked them up.

I do remember I wasn't allowed to play with Jonie after that. "Find someone else to play with," Bauma told me. I said there were no other children around, and she said, "What about Dexter Hasbrook?" So I went back to his garage.

Dexter Hasbrook never smiled, but when I did what he wanted, he stroked my head.

# - 17 -

## LIFE PRESERVER

Two and a half days before we were due to arrive in New York, the ship ran into rough weather. It was late December, so I had expected a certain amount of storm; but nothing like this. It wasn't the season or latitude for tropical hurricanes, and yet the plunging of the liner suggested we were heading straight into one.

Even when I got over my seasickness, visions of disaster kept following me around. At least I was able to fake a look of unconcern—these last months in England had rehearsed me in hiding what I felt. My final day in London, I had even managed to write Christmas cards to the cast of the play, as if cheer were natural and possible. The fact is, I was still dazed from a buffeting equal to anything the ship was taking now.

Somehow, routine persisted. A steward tapping his chimes

in the corridor announced dinner, and it occurred to me that the sensation in my stomach just might be hunger. I had not eaten all day, and images of the French Line's famous cuisine began to nag me. Holding onto the bunk with one hand, I managed to shave and dress. Then, pausing frequently to counterbalance some particularly surprising declivity and drop, I made my way up to the dining salon.

The great room was nearly vacant. Not many people had booked passage for the winter crossing anyway, and those who had were clearly not interested in food that night. The table for eight, where I had been seated at previous meals, was empty. That was fine with me; I was in no mood to talk to anyone. The *maitre d'hotel* had ideas of his own, however, and steered me toward a small table where a man my own age was sitting alone.

He acknowledged me courteously enough, rising and murmuring his name. Even so, I sensed I was intruding. As it was too late to back out now, I sat down. "Simon," which was all I had heard of his name, resumed studying his menu, and I took refuge behind mine. And so we sat. No one came to take our orders—only a few waiters had shown up for work that night. The silence at our table became conspicuous, and I told myself it was just possible the man didn't speak English. While he looked quite British—trim at forty, with impeccable tailoring, and neatly clipped sandy hair—his eyes put a doubt in my mind. Dark and brooding, they might have peered out of a bazaar at Marrakesh.

More to test his comprehension than crack his silence, I asked, "Will this be your first visit to the States?"

The ripe-olive eyes lifted for an instant. "First? Oh, not at all."

His inflection and accent were sheer Belgrave Square. So was his reserve. I made another attempt. "Going there on business?"

"Textiles," he said. His hand clamped down on his silverware to keep it from sliding about the table, and the silence resumed.

So fuck him, I thought. Let him choke on his privacy, if that's what he wants. I smiled at an empty table across the room as if returning someone's greeting, so he could see I was appreciated elsewhere, if not here.

Not until coffee did our eyes meet again. He sighed to himself, as though tyrannized by his training. "And you?" he asked. "What profession are you in?"

I faltered a moment, unsure if I still wanted to claim it. "Theatre," I said.

He turned the word over in his mind. "Actor?"

"Oh, much further down the social scale. At the very bottom. I write the damn pieces."

Only I didn't say it aloud. Actually, I was saved from answering at all by a lingering grumble from the depths of the ship. It sounded as if the entire hull was protesting the stress. I forced a smile. "Think it'll hold together?"

Impassively, he lifted his shoulders and let them drop. I recognized it instantly, the same spasm-like shrug I had been giving ever since the storm began. Who gives a damn, it said. Who cares if the bloody raft floats or sinks! I wondered suddenly if, along with being on the same ship, this man and I weren't in the same boat.

After dinner, I paused in the library, and flipped through the passenger list, hoping to find a name I knew. No one turned up, although just above my own name, I discovered a Simon Gersten. As this was the only Simon I came across, I gathered he was my reluctant dinner partner. A Mrs. Gersten was listed too, but she was still unaccounted for when I ran into him an hour later in the empty bar. Surprisingly, he asked me to join him. "Tell the barman what you drink," he suggested.

I ordered ginger ale, and then suddenly changed it to bourbon and water. Why not? The play was closed now, and I no longer needed to be on the wagon. I had never been a heavy drinker, but the wisdom of being utterly clear-headed had become apparent as soon as I arrived in London and met the director. He was a year or two younger than I, perhaps thirty-eight, fleshly, but not unattractive. He looked like a Hawaiian prince. He ranked himself not less than that, too. At a West End chop house where we went to discuss the rehearsal schedule, I lightly mentioned "someday when we've both arrived—" His head tipped back slightly. "I have already arrived," he said unsmilingly. Perhaps it was true, although I was unfamiliar with his reputation. At all events, I let the matter drop then, but privately intended to tease him about it when I knew him better.

As it happened, I never did know him any better. Although I had written *The Seashell,* my status in the production turned out to be the same as the typist who had done up the scripts. Once I had met the cast and heard the first reading, I was made to understand I would not be welcome at the rehearsals. When I persisted in coming to the theatre anyway, it might as well have been Coventry.

I would have been quite alone in London, except for the understudies. They were regarded as non-persons too, but shrugged it off with sass, and welcomed me at the pub where they gathered after rehearsal. Then even this door began to close on me. I faced down Ray, the blond understudy from Paddington, and asked him why the hospitality was cooling. "Well, you're not really one of us, Jesse," he said. "Maybe you're religious or something, but you always sit there cold sober while the rest of us are makin' drunken fools of ourselves. Makes us feel you're passing judgments on us."

For once, my clear-headedness paid off. "But how could I pass judgments on anyone?" I cried. "I'm an alcoholic! That's why I can't drink with you."

It wasn't true, but it made sense. And it worked! That night, when I joined the group at the pub, three sympathetic hands reached out to pour my ginger ale for me.

The uneven motion of the *Liberte* gave a double kick to the bourbon now, making me feel giddy; but several drinks seemed to have had no effect on Simon.

Even sitting back in his chair, with his legs crossed and a

glass in his hand, he gave the impression of standing stiffly at attention. I asked him if he had been in the army, and he almost smiled. "The RAF," he said. "But I should have been in the navy. Even when it gets bloody like this, I thrive on the sea."

"Apparently your wife does not," I said.

He examined his glass with a slight frown. "No," he replied. "She doesn't."

He finished his scotch, and signaled the barman for another. Our conversation lapsed again. For a time, I tried to carry it alone, but finally gave up, and bid him a pleasant goodnight. His glance traveled up the length of my necktie, and fixed on my chin. There seemed to be no light in his eyes at all, and I realized he must be very drunk. "You're a homosexual, I should guess," he said suddenly.

I looked at him in surprise, but did not reply. He nodded my answer for me, and added, "First of your ilk I've ever met."

"If that's true," I said, "you couldn't have gone to a very good school."

"Just Cambridge."

"Then believe me, Simon," I said, "you've met quite a few of us."

Giving a slight bow, conventional staging for an acerbic exit, I returned to my cabin. Not to sleep, of course—the wildness of the sea would have prevented that—but to lick my wounds, all of them. Around three o'clock, I apparently dozed off, and when I awoke in the morning, had coffee in my cabin as a precaution against running into Simon at breakfast.

However, the ship that had looked so vast when I boarded it in Southampton, was too small to avoid anyone for long. While I was attempting to walk along the Promenade Deck, I saw him coming toward me. I tried to pass by with lowered eyes, but he turned and fell into step beside me. "I say, old man, I'm most dreadfully sorry," he said. "About last night, I mean. I'd had a rotten setback, and I expect I was just striking out at anyone."

"Quite all right," I said, but coolly.

"Fact is," he persisted, "when I said I'd never met your kind before, I wasn't telling the truth. Had a close friend when I was eighteen, who probably was." He considered the statement, then amended it. "Who surely was. Not that he and I ever got around to anything, y'know. I was too conformist. Still am, I expect. Anyway, that's what my wife tells me."

This was more than he had said at any one time since we had met. The wonder was that he managed to get the words out consecutively, for the roughness of the sea kept us staggering away from each other until we had to link arms to get the conversation finished. "Do you still see him?" I asked. "This boyhood friend?"

He shook his head. "He was an officer on the *H.M.S. Hood* during the war."

"He was lost?"

"Nearly all of them aboard were."

"I'm sorry."

"Kind of you to say so."

Civilities took the place of conversation, but they were welcome. We parted amiably, and then kept running into each other inadvertently all morning. At the Purser's office. In the library. At noon, when I came into the dining salon, he beckoned me over to his table. Once more he was sitting alone. "Pull up a chair," he suggested.

I did, and asked if his wife was feeling any better. Once more, he made that quick hiccup of a shrug, and the familiar silence resumed. Abruptly, he looked into my face. "My wife isn't with me," he said. "She was supposed to be. She even got down to Southampton with me. But at the last moment, decided against sailing."

I murmured something, the same kind of low-key all-purpose condolence that people offer when your show closes.

"Yes," he echoed. "Rotten luck."

He seemed to lose himself in study of the menu, but apparently had forgotten why when the waiter finally came to take his order. With all the wonders of this cuisine to choose from, he asked for some barley soup and a roast beef sandwich. "My second, y'know," he said. Only for an instant did I think he meant he had had a prior lunch. "Awfully decent girl," he went on, "but twelve years younger than I. And full of all the new ideas."

We attempted another stroll after lunch, and played some cards in the smoking room; but mostly we talked, each laying out his particular rejection like a spread of solitaire. He had been married to her for three years, Margaret, nursery-named Meggie, vivacious, naturally fair-haired, a little spoiled. He could speak of little else, but she didn't seem very interesting to me. On the other hand, he could not have been much interested in backstage politics, but he listened patiently to my anger, and even showed a rush of color when I mentioned that the star of my play had been the renowned Dame Sybil Thorndike. "Oh, jolly good!" he cried. "I saw her act *St. Joan* when I was little. Really great old girl, what?"

Old? It was hard to think of her being so. Although she was far too mature for the role of the mother in *The Seashell,* and too forthright ever to be that repressive, she always convinced me she was exactly who she set out to be. It was her great gift to find the norm that exists in oddity, and the spectrum hidden in gray. Most people's first impression of her was the direct blue of her eyes, but for me it was that voice, resonant, almost rumbling, a theatre voice that kept no secrets from the top galleries. The whole cast had assembled on stage, that first morning, when we heard her coming upstairs. Two floors away, every syllable was distinct. "Of course I remember you," she was telling the doorman. "Of course, of course, I do." Everyone smiled at each other as if she were a personal achievement. Then she came out into the lights, not tall at all for someone so much larger than life.

She was always on time, always ready to go. "I get up very early," she told me once. "Play an hour of Bach at the piano to clear my mind, then give an hour of study to my lines. Or if I'm not in a show, I memorize poetry or music. It's the memory that

Dame Sybil Thorndike, with Heather Sears,
in *The Seashell*

wants its daily work-out, y'know. I'm not going to be one of those actresses who hovers up close to the prompter when I'm old." She was seventy-six then.

Seventy-six, and not wasteful of a moment that could be lived. Having just finished a year's run in a play, she took two weeks off to relax on a walking tour in Switzerland, and now plunged into rehearsal for *The Seashell.* Her focus of energy was often tiring to others, but she never made any demands for privilege, never any shows of temperament. Fifty years of stardom had taught her to keep it simple. If one of her lines needed fixing, she showed, by speaking it with too much vigor, that she was having trouble with it. "How would you rather say it, Dame Sybil?" the director asked, once. "Well," she said, "if nobody minds, I'd rather try it with no lines at all, and see if I can't say it with me old face."

To remember this now was painful, and to no purpose. I wanted to let go of it, and get on with my life. But months would probably be needed before this healed. At least knowing Dame Sybil had been rewarding. She knew I was not happy with the production, and sometimes when we were on tour, she would see me eating alone at the hotel, and ask me to her table. We never discussed the play or its evident problems, but spoke of our lives, the arts, even politics. She shared her stories of working with such disparate forces as George Bernard Shaw and Marilyn Monroe. She spoke especially of Sir Laurence Olivier, whom she had helped train, and whose career had since transcended hers. In his *Oedipus Rex*, she had played his wife/mother in a blood-red wig, a performance I would have given back teeth to have seen. She smiled when I told her so. Suddenly, she leaned across the table, and, playing her part and his too, whispered an entire scene for me. The mood of waiting doom had not left me when she straightened up. "Look," she laughed, "we've let our ice cream melt."

During the afternoon, the winds died down. "Ought to get in some exercise, now the storm's over," Simon suggested. I didn't say anything to discourage this belief, but I knew, from having lived in Florida, that such lulls only meant the eye of the storm was passing over, and that soon the winds would resume.

He and I jogged around the deck several times, and worked out in the gym. Pink-faced and sweating, Simon gave himself over to games as if to block out his own painful thoughts. He tried to teach me deck tennis, but was finally reduced to playing catch with me, inventing obstacles and handicaps for himself to make it more interesting. He was not amused when I called this "Two-handed Rugger."

"Oh, do say Rugby," he begged. "I can't bear it when people say 'Rugger'. It's like calling the Queen 'Betty'."

Simon's devotion to sports, and especially soccer, set off my obsessive backtracking again, reminding me of the leading man in *The Seashell.* He had had stage experience before, and small parts in films, but it was in this play that his name went up above the title for the first time: Sean Connery. He was not yet a world property, but there was no doubt in the cast's mind that the public would make him a major star. Quite apart from that face that made breathing so difficult when he looked you in the eye, he was a beguiling actor, honest and straight forward, with an irresistible humor. Yet on tour, everyone in the production noticed that on Monday nights, his performance never had any clout. A little investigation revealed that right after the Saturday night show, he took a train back to London so he could play ball with his pals on Sunday. His soccer team nearly always won, but the games left him so bruised that, just before performance on Monday night, he used a pain-killer. Unfortunately, this also killed the rough, warm message that made women buy tickets to see him. The stage manager gave him a talking-to, which must have been effective, because the next weekend, he forsook soccer, and channeled everything into that macho performance. Or as one of the stagehands announced in a note pinned to the backstage bulletin board: "Ball is out, balls are back!"

The storm resumed in early evening, and walking about

became hazardous—every time you put your foot down, the deck wasn't where it had been a moment before. Hoping to sleep through the worst of it, I got in my bunk early, and buckled on the harness which would keep me from being pitched onto the floor. The liner rolled so violently to one side that the drawers started rushing out of the bureau; a moment later, as we practically capsized on the other side, I would hear them slide back into place. The shuddering groans of the ship grew more ominous, suggesting that the liner was indeed breaking up. Around midnight, the steward knocked at my door, saying in French and English that all passengers were requested to report to the Cabin Class salon. It was no more than a drill, he assured, but life belts were to be worn.

I found that ropes had been strung about the salon to help passengers maneuver across the tilting deck. The piano had been strapped in place, and chairs were ingeniously buckled to the floor. I sat down next to Simon, noting that he was not wearing his life belt, but had it slung over his shoulder, cavalier style. Everyone was showing that reflex friendliness that seems to accompany this degree of uncertainty. Yet as the stress began to wear on them, characteristics became apparent that are often attributed to nationality and class. There was a certain amount of huddling together, some fumbling with rosaries, even some open despair. The Brits, however, gave that practiced appearance of calm, the men puffing at their tobacco, the women concentrating on their knitting. The Americans, conversely, made a joke of everything. Some young men from Purdue sang *Nearer My God to Thee,* mockingly off-key. Two girls from a New York fashion house hilariously modeled their life jackets with all the posturing of an *haute couture* runway. However, as the storm intensified and the laboring of the ship grew more evident, everyone seemed to retreat inside himself, and wait there for whatever would happen next.

Sitting and waiting, unable to alter our course, was the same ordeal I had had to endure in England. When the play opened out of town, the reviews had been tepid, and rightly so.

Good acting, they said, but no action. Yet the dynamics were right there, spelled out in the script: thirty minutes along, it should have been clear to the audience that the young girl had unwittingly fallen in love with her brother. None of the clues I had furnished had been staged, however, and consequently, her infatuation only became apparent late in the play, when she openly threw herself at him. Nightly, I had to stand in the back of the theatre, watching people sit up in astonishment, wholly unprepared for this action.

Fortunately, there was still time to fix it. Having worked on a number of Broadway productions, and seen two versions of this play tried out in other cities, I was ready with remedies; but they were not heard. I could never get the director to sit down and discuss them with me. We seemed to be heading for a complete wreck.

The phrase, figurative on our two-month tour of the provinces, appeared to be reality on the high seas. I glimpsed my hand gripping the arm of my chair, and my knuckles were white. Simon was buckling on his life preserver. "Odd," he said. "I had the idea I didn't care about living anymore."

Not odd, but eerie. I had been thinking the same thing myself.

Our thoughts coincided again, half an hour later, when tension in the salon seemed ready to snap. He leaned closer, speaking almost directly into my ear. "Do you ever—y'know—pray?"

I *was* praying, and his question made me self-conscious: men who can be frank about everything else, find it difficult to mention faith today. Yet all the barriers, so evident when we had met the night before, were tumbling now, and I admitted that, in these last few months, I had had to turn to prayer every day, though none of it was ever answered.

He had questions to ask about prayer, some that seemed almost naïve to me. His father had been Jewish, his mother Protestant, he explained, so both had avoided discussing religion in the home. "—almost as if it were bad form," he said. "I grew up not having the foggiest notion about all that. But there are times when one needs—I don't even know what! More than childish outcry."

A hymn by one of the Longfellows came to my mind—not the music, just some of the words, and I spoke them half-aloud. "'Thy hand in all things I behold.And all things in Thy hand—'"

"Go on," he urged. "Play the whole set!"

I did, not even sure what the words meant anymore; but the sound of them was comforting. Simon braced his elbow against mine, and after that, even when hope wavered, this point of human contact remained, reassuring to both of us, like prayer understood.

By three in the morning, the storm had pretty much spent itself, and around four, Simon and I were zig-zagging through the corridor, back to our cabins. Both of us were exhausted, and at the same time, too keyed up to sleep. "I say, you couldn't do with a drink, could you?" he said, at his door. "I've got rather a nice bottle of Moet in my suitcase. Bon Voyage, or some such."

We drank the champagne out of tooth glasses, sitting perched on the edge of the lower bunk. "Thought you rode the weather rather neatly, old Simon," I told him. He dismissed it with a wave of the hand. "Really nothing to it, after the ups and downs of textiles," he said. We did not get roaring drunk, but almost. When the bottle was empty, and I was too relaxed to move, he tossed me a blanket, then climbed up into the other bunk.

I awoke in the morning with a headache, and Simon wedged in the lower bunk beside me, both of us buck naked. He sat up suddenly. "*Good* Lord!" he said, half under his breath. His eyes turned to me. "Did anything—?"

"—-happen? Everything, I think. Don't you remember?"

He sighed and nodded. "But I was hoping you didn't."

His self-consciousness began to vanish as we dressed. The sky beyond the porthole was gloomy, but at least the sea was stable again. We had been due to dock in New York at noon, but the steward said the storm had blown the liner so far off course, we would not arrive until nightfall.

We made another stab at deck tennis after breakfast, and, in the afternoon, resumed our game of catch in the empty gym. When our eyes met, it was with some kind of humor, ironic and unspoken. It occurred to me suddenly that I was able to concentrate on something besides my failure in England. Circling the deck, we discussed dogs we had owned, books, elections, and good restaurants. We met again for drinks at five. Twilight came early, showing up the high-rise glitter of New York in the distance. He and I joined the other passengers outside on the deck to watch the always affecting entry into the harbor, with its muted tug-boat horns and great green Liberty. When the Landing Authority boat drew up to board us, always a sign that the voyage was over, I felt a pang of goodbye go through me, and a throb of welcome home. Simon's gloved hand patted my overcoat sleeve. "Cheer up," he comforted. "You'll get over all that disappointment."

It was an hour since I had even thought of it, and I wondered if somehow I wasn't already free. "I hope so," I said

"I know so," he insisted. "If I could come to terms with that Meggie business, you should be able to do as well."

"You're over Meggie then?" I asked.

"Practically," he said. "Probably a result of that bloody weather. It seemed to paraphrase everything I was feeling, only bigger and louder. Must have blown it right out of my system." He laughed. "Say what you will, that ruddy storm was a life preserver."

A steward passed by, urgently giving directions in French and English. The crowd on deck began to push toward the salons where passports would be processed. Simon and I exchanged cards and shook hands, then he strode away, glancing back as he reached the hatch, trim, even jaunty, with his faultless tweeds and improbable Casbah eyes. "I'll give you a buzz in a few days," he called. "We'll meet for a drink."

Of course we never did.

## - 18 -

## JUST THE THREE OF US

I hadn't planned to stop in Paris, but it was August again, an anniversary of sorts, and her postcard mentioned she would be there all week. I left a message at her hotel when I arrived, suggesting we meet the following noon at the usual place. There is something impertinent about calling the garden at the Palais Royal "usual," but the three of us had been there unforgettably once, and several times since to commemorate the first visit.

The garden, at least, seemed not to have changed, the pigeons strutting along the broad walks, the children shrilly at play. I paid a few francs for the use of a wire chair, and sat down by the fountain to wait. Would she and I mention him this time, I wondered? Last time, we had not. Generally, he came along anyway, invited or not. We had never found a way to ignore him for long. Despite his cool eyes and air of privacy, he seemed to pack a spotlight with him wherever he went.

Even as a child, this had been so. Gar, as I called him then, was so fair-haired, he photographed as if the camera had leaked light. At his third birthday party, he stood radiantly alone, with us other children sitting on the lawn around him in comparative darkness. He and I were frequent companions, according to a shoebox of snapshots in my attic—dressed up as clowns for Halloween, toasting marshmallows at the beach, or showing off our first long pants. His family and mine had had a tradition of friendship for four generations, so it was natural to assume that we too would be friends. And yet we were not. The fact was, I had a crush on him, something he sensed and wanted none of.

It didn't help that, as we grew up, he effortlessly took over all the things I had marked for myself. He was handsome, for instance. He was straight. He had an air of quiet authority, and the kids at high school called him The Prince. Then, to make it really difficult, he won a cup for ballroom dancing at the beach club. Next thing I heard, he and his girl were being featured as a teen dance team at a smart supper club. I would have hated him if I hadn't adored him.

While I was away at college, I read he was trying his luck on Broadway. However, the summer we were twenty-two, the war brought us both back to Los Angeles. One night, pulling up to a boulevard stop, I spied him in the car next to mine. He saw me too, but without surprise. "Want to race?" he called. We spun our tires and thrust ahead, recklessly cutting in on each other all the way to Wilshire. A police siren sounded, so we ducked into a bar. He never could handle liquor, but being competitive, ordered scotch anyway, if only to play with the ice. "Been away?" he asked.

I didn't mean to be antagonistic, but it was a way of hiding the wild hammering of my heart. "Yale," I said crisply. "Did some post-grad work there."

"Hey, did you! I played New Haven last fall."

"I know," I said, mercilessly. "I saw."

He and his dance partner had opened there in the pre-Broadway trial of a big musical starring Jessie Mathews. From overture on, it was a disaster, and totaled as Gar whirled the English star around in an adagio so steamy that her costume stained her armpits green.

Our goodbyes outside the bar were cool. He was getting ready to go into the Coast Guard, and I was waiting to be drafted. We said what everyone was saying then, "See you after the war," and yet as I drove away, an intuition that may have been just wishful thinking assured me we would meet again much sooner. Sure enough, we ran into each other at a concert, a few nights later. "I *knew* I'd see you here!" he said. "How could you possibly know?" I demanded. He shrugged and turned away, offended. It was typical of the way we always missed each other's beat.

When the war was over and my probation had been served,

I set off for New York and a new life. My mother wrote that Gar was also in New York, holed up in a hotel with stomach problems. She urged me to go see him, and with mixed feelings, I did. His glance was critical: my hair was too long, my faded jeans too tight. I retaliated by praising a current MGM musical, Metro being an especially sore point with him just then. The studio had signed him, and then used him so embarrassingly in *Till the Clouds Roll By* that he had demanded to be released from his contract. Louis B. Mayer allowed him to *buy* it back. "Took every damn cent I had," he said, with quiet rage.

"So what are you going to do now?"

"Go back to the supper clubs, soon as I can train a new partner."

"Got anyone in mind?"

He nodded. "She'll be here in a minute."

He didn't actually invite me to stay, and I didn't consciously wait. Suddenly a key ground in the lock, and she let herself in, small and blonde, with large brown eyes, and that air of independence that separates the dancer from the showgirl. She was hugging a bag of groceries, and seemed perfectly at home—chattered engagingly while she scrambled eggs in a saucer-sized electric skillet. Gar introduced her as Marjorie Belle, and said she was playing in *Beggars Holiday;* but I had already recognized her. Back when I was at Beverly High, some of my classmates had taken ballroom dancing from her father, Ernest Belcher, and she was his teen assistant. Her picture had been in the paper on a Rose Parade float, and she had modeled for the first full-length feature at the Disney Studio. Even now, I could see the artless grace of Snow White in her.

She served Gar his supper in bed, and put mine on the telephone table. There were only two plates, so she ate from the skillet, and when she had washed the dishes, asked if I wanted to walk her to the theatre. She was so lighthearted as we strolled down Broadway that I wondered if she had any depth at all; but this too appeared as she began to talk about Gar, his health, his

Marge and Gower

talent, his future. She kept enunciating his name so precisely, I had to laugh. "You sound like someone plugging a new breakfast food."

"Well, the way you say his name drives me up the wall," she said. "You make it sound like *grrr!* It has two syllables, okay? Gow-er. Gower. Gower Champion." She said this last as if trying it on for size.

After I delivered her to the stage door, I went around to the box office and bought a balcony seat. The show was not great, despite a Duke Ellington score, but Marjorie, in her little role, was funny, touching, and sexy. We had coffee together afterwards, and she told me about Gower's discovery. Low-rent apartments were still hard to come by, and rehearsal space impossible; but he had found both, and together. "Actually, it's the loft of an old church down near the Bowery," she said. "You wouldn't believe it!"

I joined her there on Sunday evening, and true enough, I didn't believe it. The church had long since been abandoned by its congregation, and was now owned by a Mr. Wu. Four flights of stairs led us up into a series of cavernous chambers, paneled, vaulted, and grimy. Gower had tried to scrub them down before he got sick, and now Marjorie was continuing the labor in her spare time. Soon, I began dropping by regularly to help. The inevitable side effect was an exchange of confidences. For protective coloration, I invented a girlfriend; but only once. It wasn't necessary with Marjorie. She seemed to like me anyway.

And I liked her. Enormously. I liked her much more than him, even with a crush on him. I was almost sorry when he got well and rejoined us. And yet, somehow, the fun didn't cease. Marjorie seemed to add the balance that had always been needed for some kind of rapport between him and me. It was tentative at first, and suffered regular reversals, but he and I finally began to enjoy each other's company. The fact that I was capable of a little basic carpentry further fused us into friendship. When our cleaning and repairing would stop for the night, the three of us would relax over a vast spread of cheese-nips and artichoke hearts. Sometimes we kicked opinions around, but just as often sat there in comfortable reverie, satisfied with the company and our own thoughts. One night, spontaneously, Gower and Margie began to dance together. There was no music, no sound even, for Houston Street below was empty, and snow had sealed the leaded casements. They whirled, whirled, whirled, light as their own shadows, and it was me who got dizzy.

Gower's concept for their act had a difference. Most other dance teams of the time presented a smooth series of breathtaking lifts, to the strains of honeyed schlock such as *Moonlight Madonna.* What Gower had in mind, however, used dialogue as well as movement—equal parts musical comedy, dance theatre, and romance. This last was inevitable, for they were so clearly in love, it communicated even when they stood still.

A great hotel in Montreal had booked them, and their opening was getting near. Marjorie left *Beggars Holiday* to give her entire focus to the act, even though her salary would have been useful just then. Orchestrations had consumed all Gower could borrow, and her costumes had yet to be made. We spent Sundays strolling among the pushcarts on Orchard Street, fingering the fine remnants, and haggling. Margie sewed up two bouffant gowns, and in the evening, the three of us sat around and *glued* sequins on the lace appliques.

On the day of their departure, Marjorie showed up at Grand Central with her hair styled a new way, and drabbed down to a conservative ash blonde. She was in high spirits, but Gower was tense. He turned to me suddenly, and lowered his voice. "Have you got any money?" I seldom did, but just this once, was carrying enough to get me through the week. He took all forty dollars. "This'll help get us there," he said. "God knows how we'll get back."

Three days later, I got an unsigned telegram from Montreal. The message was just one word. "*Smash!*" Suddenly, the rush was on. Offers came tumbling in. Boston, Washington DC, Chicago. The big hotels they played provided them with suites which usually included a couch I could adapt to. The invitation was open, and even when I couldn't really afford to, I joined them for a day or two. "Here we are again," Margie would cry. And Gower and I would add, "Just the three of us!" The remark became worn with usage, but it always convulsed us.

If my frequent presence raised some eyebrows, it also brought on a lot of kidding. "Which one are you in love with?" someone asked. I answered lightly that maybe it was their love affair I was in love with. And maybe this was true. My own romances had always flickered out quickly, and I saw no harm in warming my hands at their fire. Why not? At every performance, the patrons at their ringside tables were doing the same thing.

They were married in October, and the next night opened in New York at the elegant Persian Room of the Plaza, for the first time billed as Marge and Gower Champion. It was a stunning debut, although from the way the columnists kept emphasizing Gower's crew cut, one would have thought his barber had staged the dances. Suddenly, the team was visible everywhere—certifying the virtues of toothpaste in advertisements, appearing weekly on TV with Sid Caesar, beaming out from the cover of *Life Magazine*. It was breathtaking fun even by proxy. Still, it began forcing a question: what was my place in all this? "The Champs are traveling fast now," one friend mentioned. "Sometime soon, you've got to expect they'll leave you behind."

Inevitably, they did sign a long-term contract with MGM, and moved out to Hollywood. I told myself it was as good a time as any for me to return to my own life, and my own kind. And yet, even apart, the bond between us seemed to thrive. We wrote letters. We phoned. Sometimes they came east or I went west. Once, astonishingly, they invited me to go to Paris with them. "Compound interest on that forty dollar loan," Gower said.

Of all our good times together, it was the most meaningful to me—the one I still go back over, looking for myself and them, as in a crowded photograph. The Paris I had visited in my teens had been disappointing, but this time, I was so immediately dazzled, I could only believe it was the city that had changed. Certainly it was not a Paris I ever saw so exuberantly welcoming again. We were swarmed by French fans who had seen them in *Show Boat* or *Jupiter's Darling* and kept crying out an odd approximation of their names: March et Champion Gové.

But there was another name on everyone's lips too: Colette. The great writer was dying, our chambermaid at the hotel told us. "We must all pray for her," she said.

In lieu of prayer, but with the same intent, we bought a translation of her novel, *Cheri,* and took turns reading it aloud to each other as we went about on subway, bus, and *bateau mouche.* Remembering her long-ago kindness, I felt an almost personal loss when the fourth morning brought word of her death. Our last day in Paris, we were irresistibly drawn to the gardens of the Palais Royal, that ancient complex of theatres, boutiques, and apartments, where she had lived and was now lying in state. Everyone who had remained in town that hot August seemed to be there, waiting in patient lines on the boulevards and round and round the vast courtyard, slowly trudging by the monumental catafalque that held her. It had been draped with a silk tricoleur, which discovered every faint movement of air, and whipped out, bellied and writhed like some living thing. I still understood French poorly, and Marge and Gower not much better, yet we stood there all afternoon, listening to the eulogies, finding translation enough in the dedicated faces around us, moved by a grandeur so far from our experience. It was right, somehow, that when we left, Gower turned again to the scene and murmured as if to a star after a great performance, "We'll be back."

So here I was again, just the me of us. A surprise gust of wind swept the fountain spray over me, breaking my reverie. I glanced toward the gray stone arcades, hoping to see Marge hastening along. She was not in sight, though it was past noon. The shadows, sun-shrunk, scarcely poked out from under my chair, and low crescents of moisture lay inside my dark glasses. She would probably show no signs of discomfort in this heat. Like all dancers, she was used to sweat, and carried its glitter like a further effect of the sequins on her costume. Physical warmth was her milieu, personal warmth her gift. "You can't compete with it," Gower would say, in awe and chagrin. "They scarcely know I'm alive when she's on stage."

They returned to the theatre and to nightclubs after MGM was forced to its knees by television. Once again, we saw each other regularly, and sometimes as they toured the act, I packed my typewriter and shaving kit and joined them. Yet it wasn't quite like old times. I could not fail to sense Gower's increasing restlessness. "I want to quit dancing," he told me in Miami. "I'm pushing forty, and after that, it's all downhill for a dancer."

"What'll you do instead?" I asked. "Direct?"

He nodded. "But not just the dances. I want to stage the whole bloody show."

"What about Marge?"

His glance was wry. "Do you even have to ask? This is what she's been waiting for—the chance to start a family."

Late that year, she delivered their first son, and they named him Gregg after me. They didn't retire the act at once, however. Gregg was three before that Christmas day when Gower showed me the script of a musical comedy he had agreed to direct. Called *Bye-Bye Birdie*, it pictured the national chaos resulting from Elvis Presley's induction into the army. Marge sang some of the songs for me, and Gower explained the numbers he visualized. Flushed, animated, he looked years younger already. The next time I saw him, he appeared to have aged by decades: Rehearsal!

I was curious to see him at work, but he conspicuously did not invite me. Relentlessly a perfectionist, he never allowed himself to be judged while the work was merely 'showing progress'. Yet the sad fact was, when I finally was allowed to see a run-through, I didn't much care for the show. He sensed this as we drove cross-town in a cab, and his eyes dared me to say it. I said it: the characters were so unsympathetic, I kept losing interest. He looked away irritably, and when the cab stopped at my door, only Margie said goodbye.

It was two days before I heard from him again. "What was that crap you were saying?" he demanded on the phone. I reiterated my opinion, and he hung up. A moment later, he called back. "This is a show about kids," he cried. "You're too old to understand." It was me who hung up this time. Minutes later, I phoned back. Off and on, we argued for an hour, and the next morning, met for breakfast to toss around ways of humanizing the characters. This was so productive that eventually he had me travel with the show on its out-of-town try-out as his unofficial devil's advocate.

Notices were mixed when *Birdie* opened in New York, but the times were more favorable than *The Times,* and a younger generation made the show an enormous hit. Gower was suddenly catapulted into almost unreachable prominence. He was applauded when he entered restaurants, his phone rang full-time despite a secret number, and the foyer of his apartment was choked with the scripts of musicals and plays sent around for his consideration. "He'll change now," people predicted. "They always do." But I saw no difference in him at this point. When he began work on his next show, *Carnival,* he asked me once more to go out of town with the production as his sounding board. "I've reached a point where people only tell me what I want to hear," he said. "I need someone that I can't fire to argue with me."

It is possible that he came to regret this invitation. Perhaps we both did. I kept picking at what I felt were weaknesses in the new production—lines that didn't pay off or story points that weren't clear. Occasionally, he made use of the alternatives I suggested, but more often, in struggling to explain to me why my proposals were sheer nonsense, he would force the right solution out of himself. It was what I was being paid to do, but it put a terrible strain on our friendship.

And there were other strains. Marge had stayed in New

York to take care of Gregg, and in her absence, Gower became infatuated with his leading lady. Sweet-voiced and wide-eyed, she had an air of great vulnerability, perfect for the role she was playing. Off-stage, she was capable of seething scenes, although the words she and I exchanged on Easter Sunday were much exaggerated in the re-telling.

"I know how destructive it can be," Mike Stewart, the red-haired writer of *Carnival* sympathized.

"How destructive *what* can be?" I demanded.

"Jealousy."

"*Jealousy!*" I protested. "I was just standing up for Marge!"

Undeceived, he met my eyes. "Of course," he said.

I never discussed the matter with Gower—our old communication had seemed blocked, of late—and how much of the gossip reached home, Marge never indicated. She looked particularly lovely on opening night in New York, however, and the photographers, waiting for a confrontation between the two women at the party afterwards, had to be content with flashes of them smiling at each other. "All the same," said one interested bystander, "there'll be repercussions, you can count on that."

The only repercussion I could see was that the Champions' second son, Blake, was born about nine months later. I worked much more happily for Gower on *Hello, Dolly*, and to celebrate its astonishing success, the three of us visited Greece together. I went into hock for this, since we rented a yacht and cruised around the Aegean Islands, eating artichokes every day, forming a thirst for wine with a pine flavor, and singing "Hello, Dolly" in Greek. (*Yasu, Kukla!*) Squint lines I had never noticed before became visible against my suntan, and my hair began to show gray. Actually, it had begun turning while I was still in college, but since then, a handy chemical had helped me lie about my age. I scarcely bothered with the messy procedure during our cruise, just as Gower did not trouble to shave. To his dismay, however, his beard was coming in grizzled. Not to worry, I told him, and bought a patent hair dye at an island dispensary. It smelled like brimstone, but quickly restored our color and self-image. It did, at least, until we went up on deck again, and Marge screamed with laughter. In the bright May sunshine, my hair and his beard had turned green.

He called me to join him during the pre-Broadway tour of his next production. My mother had just died, and he thought it would help to plunge me into work. The hours were long, and he was under enormous pressure, yet we had never been so close. *I Do, I Do* was a complete musical comedy, but without chorus line or change of set, and only two characters. Mary Martin and Robert Preston played them brilliantly, and the words and music were delightful, but to Gower's mind, something was still lacking. This story of a marriage from the wedding night on, was full of wonderful foreplay, he said, but never quite got around to a climax. I suggested that he find the solution in the study of his own marriage. Dubiously, he tried it, and when it proved useful, continued to sort through his life, finally speaking of things he had never told me about: his father's desertion, and the genteel poverty he consequently grew up in; the rivalry with his brother, his resistance to his mother's unyielding demand for excellence. And yet, just when I would think I was finally beginning to understand him, I'd discover that for every door he opened, another would somehow edge shut. He said it all, one day, when he asked me to buy him some toiletries, and, unasked, I included a deodorant. "Are you telling me something?" he asked.

I nodded: "You smell like rehearsal."

He laughed. "Then it's lucky nobody gets very close to me."

It probably wasn't a remark meant for careful scrutiny, but it kept bumping around my mind over the next two years, sometimes reminding me that he had been more open with me than I had with him. I had, for instance, never told him or anyone about my arrest. And now suddenly it was too late for confidences. I was at work on a book, and so did not go on tour with his next production—saw it only when it began giving previews just before the Broadway opening. It was not the right time to make suggestions—he was as tense as a sprinter on his mark—but I offered some anyway in a dingy little bar after the performance. This time, the sharp line between criticism and remedy seemed to cut too close, and abruptly he arose from the table. "This used to be helpful," he said crisply, "but I can't listen to it anymore."

All communication stopped, and neither of us seemed to know how to start it up again. It was Marge who eventually engineered an accidental meeting. He and I immediately began kidding and pounding each other's arm. However, we never really talked about his work again.

Suddenly, the three of us were fifty. We met in Malibu, and for the first time, I brought along someone who mattered to me. Everyone liked him immediately, and yet, somehow, it changed the mixture. Gower, slim and silvering now, was gracious, but remote, perhaps preoccupied by preparations for the film he was planning to produce and direct. There was little time for us to catch up on each other, but as if to make up for it, he sat me beside him at the huge birthday bash he threw for Marge. Towards one o'clock, when the candles on the cake had been blown out and the rock combo temporarily silenced, Gower lifted his glass and spoke quietly, ardently, in tribute to Marge. It had been a love affair, he said—was a love affair still.

And yet, within a few years, they were apart. I was out on the West Coast again, doing the screenplay for a book I had written, and heard the details from each. It was familiar stuff. Home and children had taken her in one direction, career had swept him far out in another. Their house was up for sale, and I helped Marge sort and pack, a reverse image of the time we had cleaned out the rectory in the abandoned church.

Gower had already moved into an empty crag-top mansion that had once belonged to Charles Boyer. At the push of a button, the roof of the formal dining room could slide back to reveal the sky; and from the garden wall that precariously encircled the estate, he could look down on his neighbors sunning themselves far below. Lofty, isolated, he seemed to have set himself up in some kind of metaphor.

We still saw each other when he came East, but never very satisfactorily. There wasn't a whole lot we could talk about now, the past being off-limits, and his current output requiring the utmost in tact. *Prettybelle. Sugar. Mack and Mabel.* Vacant lots in a posh neighborhood, the critics indicated.

He married again, a handsome young woman, who encouraged us to resume our old companionship; but without the balance Marge had supplied, he and I began to slip back to the petty needling that had marked our adolescence. Temporarily, Gar took over a leading role in a Liza Minelli musical, but I learned of it from a newspaper, rather than from him. Stung at being excepted, I didn't go to see his performance. In response, he did not come to see a show I had adapted, then at the Booth Theatre. I made up my mind to let the friendship lapse, but the timing was wrong for that. Now that his career was beginning to falter, too many other people were abandoning him. The fashionable seers were even now predicting that one more flop would finish him forever. Heedlessly, he sank everything into an iconoclastic rock version of *Hamlet.* It was so calamitous as to be magnificent—rawly creative, mammoth, but even at its most imaginative, offensive. I saw it twice, sweating, clenching my muscles in an effort to make it work. It did, magically, in the final duel scene, but the first-nighters shuffled their feet, and were silent only when it came time to applaud.

I went backstage to see him afterwards. He was standing alone, wearing the red jacket he always wore on opening nights. He listened impassively as I told him the things I liked about the show, but then an impossible silence fell between us. After a moment, he took a breath and began backing away. "I have to see some friends," he said.

Too proud for sympathy, too bruised to roll with the punches, he went back to his mountain-top isolation in California. I too was in process of leaving the city, moving a hundred miles out on Long Island. I saw Marge often, but did not hear from Gower, or even about him, until a few years later, when a mutual acquaintance phoned. Incredibly, he said, Gower was hammering at the gates again—a big new musical was already in rehearsal. "But he's pretty run-down physically," he added. "Might perk him up if you dropped by, like you used to." But by now, "used to" had been used up.

There was another phone call five weeks later, this time from Marge. "Gower's in the hospital," she said. "You'd better come."

I took a train to New York and joined her. In a traffic-locked taxi, she explained Gower's condition, but the medical terms had neither meaning nor immediacy for me. Visiting hours were over by the time we got to the hospital, so I left a note saying I would be back the next day. His new show, *Forty-Second Street*, was due to open on Broadway that night, but I had not planned to go. Margie found a ticket for me, however, and I managed to borrow a tux.

Being late August, it was still daylight when we entered the theatre. The first-night crowd was dazzling, but with a hard, show-me attitude. Suddenly, before the show had even begun, everyone was jolted into applause. Instead of an overture, a hundred tap shoes and a rehearsal piano began thunderously banging out a basic routine from behind the curtain. The backstage world of the early Thirties that this opened upon presented Gower at his most certain. Never patronizing the grand cliché of this show-biz fable, he blazoned it with wit, tenderness, and imagination. Long before intermission, he had climbed back to the pinnacle of his profession, and at the triumphant final curtain, the cheers and bravos almost made up for the damnation of *Hamlet*. It was then that the producer came out on the stage to tell the audience, the cast, and especially the media, that Gower was dead.

I kept waiting for regret to hit me, but it didn't. Not when I read the accounts of his death on the front page the next day, not when I went to the huge memorial for him at the Winter Garden Theatre, not when I saw the lights of Broadway turned off for a moment in his memory. The fact is, I felt nothing at all, but the surprise of feeling nothing.

It was nearly one o'clock when Marge came hurrying up the broad quad-rangle of the Palais Royal garden, clutching the smartly wrapped packages that would furnish her an excuse for being late. Her hair was gleaming and newly short, and her eyes bright with humor—the kind of woman who will frankly tell you her age, but won't look it. "—couldn't resist this beaded purse," she was saying. "And look at these little shirts for my grandson!"

As the excitement of reunion wound down, we wandered through the cool arcades, not consciously trying to remember, but unable to forget the day when, along with half of Paris, the three of us had come here to pay our respects to the great novelist. I could not help contrasting those two highly public leave-takings. Colette's name had grandly outlived her death, but Gower's already seemed to be dimming. *Forty-Second Street* was still playing in New York, one of the longest runs in theatre annals, but the producer had begun taking sole credit for its success. Another director was now reigning supreme over the musicals, and the show-business historians had found new champions. Time does that sort of thing. But it can also cure.

Maybe the healing had been going on without my realizing, and only now was I aware of it: a naturalness in thinking of him once more. Hindsight was handy, and even clear. Remarks I hadn't picked up the first time around began to seem like minor rosebuds. A feeling of closeness was there again, and when Marge and I glanced at each other, I knew she felt it too. Her face was so luminous, I wanted to ask if she was still in love with him. Then it occurred to me, that she could be asking me the same question.

It was something she and I had never discussed. Nor did we now. Or need to. She slipped her arm through mine, and, sometimes talking, sometimes silently musing, we strolled back through the garden, and out into the mid-day rush of rue de Beaujolais.

## - 19 -

## THE DEGAS LOOK

I caught the last plane out of New York that night. The flight was not easy. I could not rest for the images of Noo that kept crossing my mind. These, at least, did not hurry. In my thought, she took her time showering, then brushed her hair till it shone, and only at last opened the plastic bottle. It was half full of capsules, and she took them all; Washed each one down with a sip of water. "All gone," I imagined her saying, the phrase she had used in her baby days when she had finished her meal. Then she lay back in bed and turned off the light.

Her husband met me at the airport and drove me to the hospital. He had let her sleep late that morning, he told me—a little extra rest would do her good. At noon, he had knocked at her door, and when there was no answer, entered. The room was dark, silent except for the labored breathing. He spoke her name, then shook her shoulder. A moment later, he was dialing 911.

She still wasn't out of danger when they brought me to her side. She was not conscious, and her color was like tallow, but at least her breathing was more regular. No note had been left behind to explain her action. An intern had stapled a blue paper bracelet around her wrist with all her statistics, yet I had to face the fact that I didn't know who she was anymore.

She was eight years younger than I, and named after our grandmothers, Jean and Ellen. Pronunciation of these was too complex for her early efforts, so she called herself Nini. Inevitably, Sharly and I exaggerated this into Noonoo, but usage soon reduced it to Noo. She was an enchanting child—blond and snub-nosed, with the long, straight eyelashes of a horse. Our mother and father didn't want me or Sharlie to feel left out so they made us her god parents. Of course we overdid

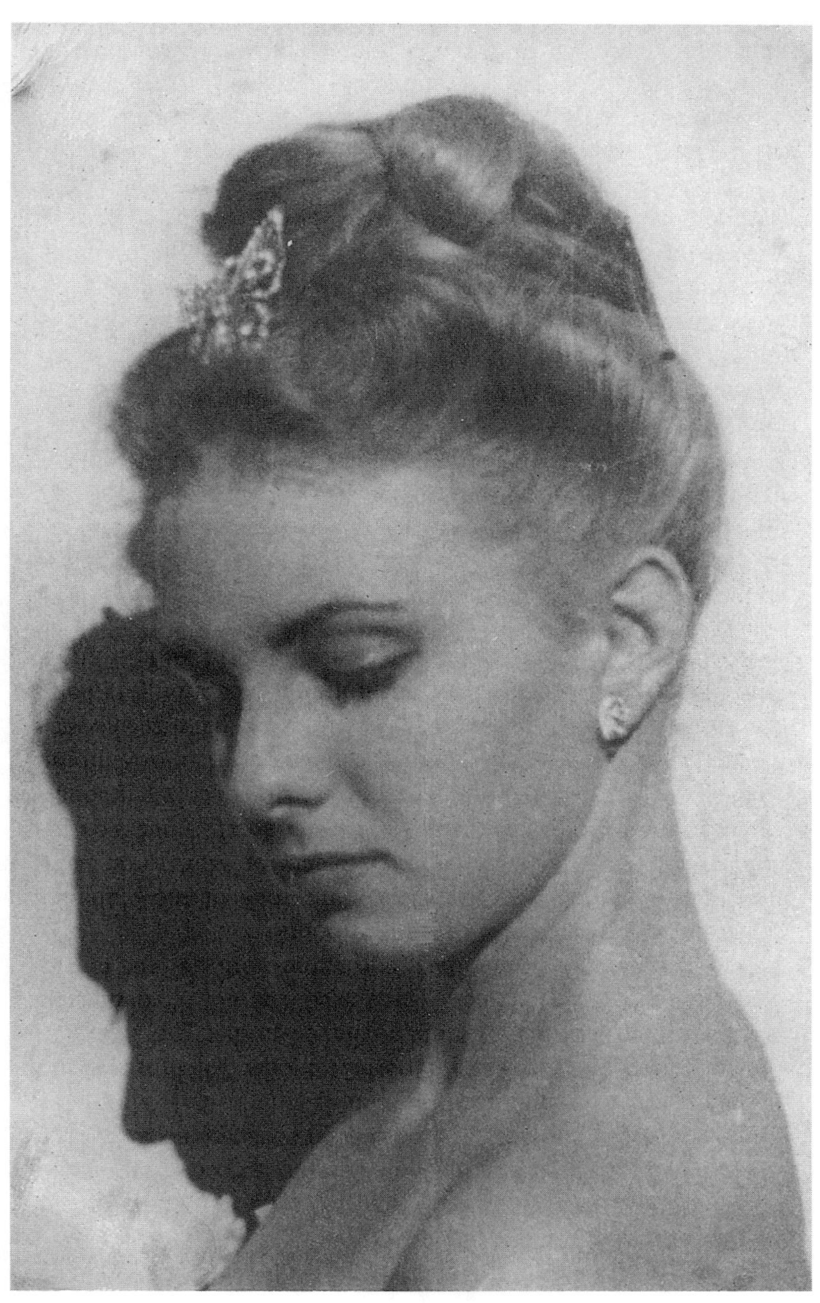

Noo at fifteen

this—doted on her in the way that smothers Easter chicks. Literally hand- fed her. "I do it by myshef," Noo would eventually protest. That's the problem of being the baby of the family, I suppose—everyone wants to live her life for her.

I don't mean that she was putty in our hands. She had a stubborn streak that would show up inconveniently. Fearless too—held out her hands to the most scurvy-looking animals. And once when she was eleven, she swam across the bay from our summer house on Balboa Island. Didn't tell anyone she was going, and took no one with her. Some fishermen picked her up when she'd swum nearly the whole distance. She gave them no more explanation than we got now about the sleeping pills.

I came to see her at the hospital every day that week. Gradually, she fumbled back into consciousness, and on the third afternoon, when I sat down by her bed, she knew me, and whispered, "Hello, Buddy." Mostly, we just smiled and nodded at each other, but long before I actually asked her, the air was loaded with the question. "Why did you do it, baby?"

I said it softly, but the nurse picked it up. "Now, now, we're just going to talk about happy things."

So that's what we talked about—good times, mostly childhood. The snap-shots I had taken of Noo growing up find little to agree upon. In one, she is gangling and big-toothed with her blond hair tinctured green from the swimming pool. In another, she's plump and simpering, looking rather like a cloud of luminous gas. But when I came back to Los Angeles after graduating from college, I found a fourteen-year-old beauty—tall, fair-haired, and dreamy-eyed. She had changed her middle name to Vivian in tribute to Scarlett O'Hara, who was also responsible for her way of looking up at a man through her lashes.

I began going berserk with the camera—Noo pensive in the garden, Noo in tennis togs, Noo on horseback. The images glowed with her youth, but after the twenty-third batch, "glow" got kind of stale. I varied it by snapping her in old Halloween wigs with blacked-out teeth, grotesque travesties that we topped off with nonsense stolen from radio shows.

Me: *"Are you Rubiyat LaTrine or the Countess di Rumpf?"*
Noo*: "I sure am, honeychile."*

It was not very funny, but it never ceased to break us up. A better set-up was inspired by a black evening gown that Sharlie had left behind when she got married. My photographs of Noo dressed up in it copied the glamorous artifice of fashion magazines back then. Not anywhere in nature could you find the mouth I painted over her lips. And the eyes! only in the royal tombs of Egypt. "Is that me?" she asked Matt when she saw the proofs.

Matt usually helped me take these photos. My closest companion and artistic ally, he had wonderful ideas about dramatic lighting, which he borrowed from Twentieth Century-Fox, where he was under contract. It was I, however, who developed the Degas look. I say develop, but actually, it was the product of my incompetence. Either my camera was out of focus, or the tripod got jarred, but the resultant images of Noo were hazy, romantically unreal. We began to emphasize this. Just as I'd click the shutter, Matt would spur that dreamy look of hers by whispering, *"You're in love!"* Actually I think she was. With Matt, of course. Well, perhaps I was too.

Blond, and twenty-one, Matt had all the advantages of perfect features. When we would walk into a night club, I'd notice how every head turned to look at him—-it was almost as good as being handsome myself. But Matt was never self-conscious about it. Being on show was his career, something the actors' agents all encouraged. What the agents didn't encourage however, was his always being with me. Boys going out with boys wasn't good for his image, they complained—could wreck his chances in films in the fans caught on. "I got a note from the Pope today," he told me—that's what he called the head of the agency. "He says if I don't have a regular girlfriend to trot around, he'll assign me a starlet."

Both of us groaned at that idea. If we were going to be stuck with a smoke screen, we wanted one who would be fun. None of the young actresses we knew were quite right for the role, however. She would have to be someone with class Someone who wouldn't try to take over. And most especially, one who wouldn't be too knowing about our relationship. Matt frowned thoughtfully. "What about Noo?" he asked.

"Come off it," I said. "She's only fourteen."

"You'd never guess it," he said, nodding at one of our fashion pictures.

"Anyway, Mom'd never allow it."

"But it won't be for real," he argued. "It's only for appearance. And after all, you'd be along. Where could you find a better chaperone?"

That, in fact, was the clinching argument I gave my parents, and the next Friday, Matt and I took Noo to a big charity do in Beverly Hills. She wore one of Sharlie's cocktail dresses, but still looked like a kid dressed up until we smeared a touch of silver on her eyelids. And there was nothing childlike about the way she responded when some publicist wanted to snap a picture of her. "Please," she murmured, practically Garbo, "no photographs."

It worked like a dream. Or nearly. My father grumbled about his baby growing up so soon. And my screenwriter friend, Ellis, invoked Freud, warning of unseen consequences. But the agents were satisfied. Letting people think that Matt was engaged to my sister was the perfect excuse for him and me always being together. "Ought to have another girl along to make it look really kosher," suggested Carole, a young and knowing divorcee. Sometimes, she came with us, but it was more fun when we kept it just a family unit.

The Mocambo was the most glamorous of the clubs on Sunset Boulevard, and an essential place for Matt to be seen, but we kept having to get Noo home by midnight since we usually said we were only going to a movie. However, we gradually expanded this lie into the popular teen-age ruse of slipping her out the back door after she had told our parents she was going up to bed. There was no harm in this deception, Matt and I assured each other—what Mother and Dad didn't know wouldn't hurt them. Or Noo either. She guessed nothing about Matt and me-—not for some decades would the mysteries of queerdom become common knowledge among adolescents, or, for that matter, grown-ups. All she knew was, she got to go dancing, see celebrities, and be with the boy she adored. When some of her classmates bragged about going to the prom at the Black Fox Military Academy, she was able to drop in a mention of Ciro's, or the new Kit-Kat.

We took her to all of them. Bishop's, for instance. It was way downtown, sort of a home away from home for jazz musicians, so smoky you couldn't tell who was dancing with who. Noo liked it because once Lana Turner told her she loved her dress. But she liked the Baroque too, because whenever we came in, the pianist would slyly sneak in a phrase of *Oh, You Beautiful Doll*—though whether in tribute to her or Matt I could never determine. "Act as if you're used to it," I always told her; and she glided through these evenings, smiling but slightly apart, like someone in the future trying to remember this moment.

Most exciting, because it was most dangerous, was the Clover Club, a starkly modern building that crouched on the hillside above the stretched-out glitter of Los Angeles. Except nobody went up there for the view. Rumor was, there was gambling upstairs, and drugs could be had; but it was the era of hiding everything, and the management devised its own smoke screen by making the downstairs appear to be the in-place for the younger set—-featured the music we liked, usually waived the cover charge, and really courted us.

The maitre d', especially. Jorge. He was a little gray-haired Filipino who always found a table for us right in the center of things. After our second visit, we never had to order again: he automatically brought over our drinks, scotch for Matt and me, and a wicked looking ginger ale with two cherries for Noo. Everyone called him George, but she was taking first-year Spanish at school, and pronounced his name correctly. It sounded like she was clearing her throat, but he adored it—was always kidding that he was going to steal her away.

And one night, we thought he had. The music suddenly got so loud we couldn't hear, and Jorge barreled over to our table and grabbed Noo's wrist. He dragged her through the service door into the kitchen, and down a corridor that was just chicken-wire and plaster. Matt and I caught up with them as he was shoving open a metal fire door. A warning light flashed on, and he shoved us out into a dark alley. "You not come here no more, or I telephone papa" he yelled, and slammed the door on us.

We didn't understand until the next morning when we saw the newspaper—some gangster had been polished off in the foyer, and the cops had moved in quickly, demanding to see everyone's identification. "Hope you weren't too scared by all that," Matt said. But Noo shook her head. "I loved it," she said. She was still calling it the greatest night of her life, three or four years later.

By that time, Matt and I had become merely friends. However, he continued to take Noo out dancing, or to social occasions where it was important to be seen with someone charming, young, and female. Some of the other young actors we knew had begun dating her too, all of them personable and handsome. Our mother was delighted that her youngest was so popular, and Noo, herself, adored the young men's attention—very week, was in love with another of them. "Just in love, y'know," she told Ellis. "Nothing more serious."

"Ah," he said, with his half-hidden mockery, "I'm glad it's not more serious than love." He was fond of her in his studied way, and often reproached me for what he called her protective services. "Are any of these dates of hers straight?" he asked me. "Is a single one of them heterosexual?"

"Maybe not."

"Does she know that?"

"I shouldn't think so."

His transparent eyebrows lifted. "And she's how old now?"

I got uncomfortable. "Sixteen, seventeen, I don't know."

"At all events," he said, "too old to be playing with *paper dolls*."

He could speak more plainly than that, however, and before long, did. We ran into each other by the pool of director Billy Wilder, who I was trying to interest in a story of mine. Apparently Ellis was there to interest Wilder in a story of *his*, and there was a sudden tension between us. He asked after Noo, and took offense when I replied inattentively that she was busy that day.

"Ah?" he said. "Camouflaging which notable young queer?"

I was attentive now, all right, and faced him. "Not very funny!"

"I quite agree," he said. "Rather sad, in fact. Some people might consider that you've turned her into a junior fag hag."

He made no pretense of listening to my angry denial. "Indeed, some might say you've used her as drag," he continued. "Dressing her up in all the glitz you don't have the courage to put on yourself—surrounding her with all the young men you're attracted to, but are afraid what people 'll think—trying to live out your fantasies through her."

"That's not so," I cried.

He shrugged. "By the time you discover it is, it'll be too late for her."

Our friendship did not recover soon, but I did not dismiss what he had said. While most of his accusations seemed too absurd to even consider, they left me feeling uneasy for Noo. This nagged me until I was forced to do something about it. I won't say I phoned Central Casting, but by the end of the week, I had rounded up some very attractive young men, all of them guaranteed straight as an arrow, and set up some beach picnics and impromptu barbecues where they could meet her.

Somehow it didn't work. She had fun at these parties, and enjoyed romping in the surf with the vigorous young men, but she was not used to their hot-handed play once the campfire died down. As a result, whenever there was a choice, she chose to be with softer boys who chatted about ballet or music, conferred about her clothes, and left her at her door with a harmless kiss on the cheek.

Perhaps this pattern changed when she went east to college—I cannot be sure, since I was consciously drawing away from her now. However, she wrote enthusiastic letters about her studies, the proms she went to, and especially the plays she was cast in. Eventually, one of her former escorts recommended her to a troupe of touring actors, and she left college to travel about the Midwest and New England, playing Shaw, Shakespeare, and Oscar Wilde at schools, women's clubs, and town halls. Sharlie and my mother held their breath unnecessarily—they had heard the usual stories about men setting snares for young actresses. But Noo was never safer, according to Maggie, the troupe's character woman.

"She wasn't responsive to boys from the colleges we played," she told me later. "They were too rough and too hot. She much preferred being with one of our more artistic actors, until I explained a few genetic subtleties she'd been missing. I suppose that's what turned her attention to older men."

"Older men?"

"Guys in their forties and fifties," she said. "By that age, they're more appreciative, more willing to make concessions to the kind of poetic romancing she likes. A lot gentler than the jocks, and infinitely more relevant to a girl than—" She hesitated, then met my eyes frankly. "—than you gay guys."

The man Noo married when she was twenty-two was exactly twice her age. He was a quietly handsome drama professor with a daughter almost as old as herself. They honeymooned in Italy, and then settled down on a small Southern campus. From time to time, I visited them, but found her to be quite unlike my old Noo. Gone was the glamorous grooming I had instigated—-she was plump, pretty, and suburban now—but the change I sensed was less visible. "Are you all right?" I finally asked. "Are you happy?" She nodded and smiled and found another subject to chat about.

They moved often, finally returning to California, and it

was here that she gave me a clue. I was in Hollywood writing a film, and she drove into town to see me. As we strolled her ungainly dog around the block, she referred obliquely to some change she was experiencing. "What kind of change?" I asked. A sudden uneasiness made me camp it. "Aren't we a little young for *change a vie?"*

She shrugged and smiled, but it was not her old smile: her lips pressed tensely against her teeth now. Privately, I asked her husband what was troubling her, but his answers were discreetly vague: winter always depressed her, she'd had a cold, etc. The night before I returned to New York, however, he said suddenly, "It's as if she's grieving over something."

"Like what?"

"I don't know. I'm not sure she does either." He shook his head. "Like a kid who can't find her way home."

For over a year, she scarcely wrote to me, though she would talk on the phone if I called her. Usually, that is. Once, in answering, she faked a voice and said she was not at home. Generally, she seemed pleased to hear from me, but became a stranger if I asked questions. She spoke a great deal about prayer, and often about old times, "back when everything was so simple." I had no idea how serious it was until I got the phone call that she had tried to take her life.

Suddenly, I found my fingerprints all over the scene. Every one of them seemed to name me as an accessory before the fact. "That's not so!" I had cried out to Ellis, long before; but on the plane, in the taxi, in the hospital corridor, I struggled against my own attack—accused myself of carelessly steering her in all the wrong directions, setting her up with values as blurred and unreal as that fake Degas look we used to strive for. With the training I'd given her, it was no wonder she had found it impossible to deal with ordinary life.

There seemed no way to ground my self-imposed lightning, for we were never alone together. Her husband was always there, or Sharlie, or the nurse. Not until my last night in Los Angeles did I find a chance. By way of therapy, her doctor had put her in charge of one of the other patients, a confused old party in a wheelchair. "Walk with me while I give him his exercise," she told me. "We can talk while I push him along the corridor here."

We strolled in silence while I tried to steady my voice. The first word I blurted must have revealed my torment, however, because she cut in at once. "It's not your fault, Buddy," she said. "It's not anyone's fault. The depression I've been fighting these past years—there's a physical cause for it, the doctors tell me. A chemical imbalance in my system—that's what has been to blame. But there's a medication for it now, and— Well, anyway, I'm going to be all right."

Whether I believed what she said—whether I even understood it—I cannot say now, for the old man in the wheelchair twisted around just then, and peered up at her. "Which nurse are you?" he demanded, querulously. "Beth or Elsie?"

"I sure am, honeychile," she said, shooting me a droll glance.

For that moment, anyway, we could not stop laughing.

## - 20 -

DEAN B.

"It happen in the wink of an eye," my father's housekeeper told me. "Right there settin' in church." She pressed the folded handkerchief against her face, blotting the tears that kept coming. "When I tells folks about it, they think I just makin' the whole thing up."

My sisters and I came back to the little college town at once, two of us from far away. The big Southern-style house he had so resolutely kept open and hospitable since my mother's death seemed empty and echoing now; but only for the first few minutes were our voices hushed. However somber the occasion, the three of us were glad to be under one roof again—we had remained close despite the distance our lives had put between us. Yet some element of sibling rivalry must have remained, for on the third day, when the lawyer arrived and we sat down to lunch, I had a premonition that my father had left his estate to the girls.

My hunch had a lot to back it up: both sisters had fulfilled their obligations to him lovingly and with great dedication. Sharlie had been born with his keen sense of business, and was always available to discuss his ideas, while Noo, warm-hearted and shining-eyed, had kept my mother's tradition of comfort for him. My own contribution had not been in the same league. I could sometimes make him laugh, and he was touched when I dedicated my first novel to him; but largely, I had not lived up to his expectation. I had never shared his intense interest in the surge of the Dow, or the five-yard gain in inter-collegiate football. Worse, I had never gotten married or had any children, and the family name he loved was ending with me. He had asked no questions, but all the same, an important one had waited there between us. Some old puritan ethic kept telling me I hadn't earned a whole lot of consideration now.

Alberta brought in the covered dish of green-bean salad, and served the lawyer as she would have my father, generously heaping his plate. "This was his favorite lunch," she told him. "This, with a glass of Orvieto white wine. And some apple pie. 'Alberta,' he say, 'just serve it to me in a pail.'"

The lawyer smiled and nodded deferentially to the head of the table. The chair there was not occupied, though it might as well have been, so persistently felt was the old man's courteous manner with its lurking waggishness. Above the dining room door was the sign he had had one of his grandsons paint, and to which he wordlessly pointed when criticized for his enjoyment of the table. *To Hell with Diet,* it said. Yet for a man of his age and intake, he had stayed surprisingly trim. In the caricatures he

A passport picture of my mother,
father, and Noo.

sometimes drew, he presented himself as a stick with a mustache. The actuality was more pleasing: he was handsome in an unremarkable way, with eyes blending green and tan, and hair that, for most of his life, not only remained brown, but remained. While in these last years, his skin seemed to have belonged to someone slightly larger, he still resembled the man I first remember.

Even though I have enviable recall, my early memories of him are few, and most of these colored by my resistance. In his reasonable way, he was a very insistent man. Every morning, he would brush my hair straight back, buttering it down with something called Sta-comb, determined to make it lie flat like his did; but a few minutes later, the entire sticky mass would slowly rise up, and then flop back over my brow. The same kind of involuntary stubbornness defeated him in other ways. His efforts to teach me to play ball came to nothing. He strained to communicate his passion for automobiles, but apparently I was always thinking of something else. Movies, probably. My nurse, May-May, had discovered the best way to get a little peace was to take Sharlie and me to the films, and I responded to them as if my eyes had opened on the real world at last. My father, who did not share this fascination, told me long after that, on a drive to Santa Monica when I was five, I gave him a run-down of John Barrymore in *Beau Brummell* that went on for two hours, detailing every plot twist, describing every costume, surviving every effort to change the subject.

He and I kept missing each other's message till I was almost ten. Christmas was only a few days off, and out of a full heart, I had decided to make my mother's gift myself. Finding some wooden coat hangers in her closet, and an unopened can of jade green house paint in the garage, I set to work. It shouldn't have been difficult, but the brush kept leaving loose hairs that I couldn't always tweeze off with my fingers. I finally solved the problem by tossing the brush away and dipping each coat hanger directly into the paint can, first one end, then the other, counting on the two tides of green to ooze together in the middle. I had planned to give twelve of these to my mother, but by the time I had finished eight, most of the paint seemed to be on the garage floor and myself. I don't know how it had managed to soak into my shirt and shoes, but since I had sneaked a pee in the bushes, there was tell-tale green on my fly, with maybe a more disconcerting condition behind it. I tried cleaning my hands with the garden hose, but water didn't help, and neither did soap. Beginning to suspect I was in trouble, but hoping to pass it off as a joke, I romped indoors. Ida, our cook, did not return my grin when she saw those sticky jade tracks on her kitchen floor. Her own heavy footfall sounded through the house as she went to summon my father. "Oh, God," he groaned, when he saw the garage. "Like a massacre! Only *green!*"

I knew from past experience what his displeasure could mean. He had spanked me for no worse cause than kicking Sharlie in the stomach, so he would probably cut my head off for this. To my surprise, however, he tried an approach that was radically different. Talking reasonably, he located a tin of turpentine, and cleaned me up. Shoes, shirt, and corduroys were hidden in a trash can, and the wide puddles of paint swept thin with a broom until they all blended together. We would have, he said, the first jade green garage floor in Los Angeles.

He did not tell my mother. At dinner, that night, she noticed a faint hovering of turpentine, but he claimed not to smell anything, and gave me a wink. The secret we shared did not immediately revolutionize our relationship—I continued to resist when he tried to teach me fractions, and he still pressed for the last word in any argument. All the same, it was the beginning of trust between us. Conversations began happening, and I found he often had good solutions when I went to him with a problem. Perhaps this could have developed into the kind of rapport that binds father and son forever, but in my fifteenth year, I plunged as if programmed into a life too secret to share with him.

"—the letters he'd dictate to his own kids always sounded like business correspondence," Sharlie was telling the lawyer.

She got laughing, and Noo filled in: "—even ending them, 'I remain, yours sincerely—'"

She started laughing too, and Sharlie picked it up again. "Signed them with his first name and middle initial. Dean B. And that's what we came to call him, once we were old enough to think 'Daddy' sounded babyish—"

My sisters kept topping each other with memories of him, and even Alberta paused by the swinging door to share a story. It was she who had given him the will to live after my mother's passing; had babied him, bolstered him, sometimes even bossed him. Plump, brown, richly maternal, she seemed to number him among her children, and the open affection between them had discouraged the ladies who had hoped to find in him a brief, but profitable, alternative to widowhood. The resultant gossip had been astonishing to both of them. "But he just say, 'Alberta, considerin' my years, it's a damn fine compliment!'"

I sat silent during these reminiscences, only beginning to realize I had been so involved in keeping Dean B. from knowing about me, I hadn't really gotten around to knowing him.

And yet he leapt to life, suddenly and with a pang, whenever I came across something that had been peculiarly his. Just before lunch, I had glanced into his office, and my mind automatically filled him in at his old roll-top desk. Heedless of his retirement, he had worked there every day in deep concentration, his glasses swinging open-bowed from the cord around his neck, his shirt pocket spotted with dots of ink from his ballpoint pen, his index finger encircled by a rubber band to remind him of some task. "Such as what?" I asked.

"Maybe to pray for a shred of intelligence in the White House," he replied. He might have been kidding. I could not always tell.

It was in his study, surrounded by charts, graphs, and stacked issues of the *Wall Street Journal*, that he was most at home. "Won't you step into the office?" he would say, an invitation offered so frequently that his grandsons could steal a laugh by mimicking it. Sooner or later each day, almost everyone in the family pulled a chair up to his desk to confer with him. Neighbors too, or students from the nearby campus. Even workmen on the premises. They were likely to call him by his first name, believing Dean to be his position at the college. The man who delivered the bottled water once told me about stopping by for payment due, "—and the old dean gets me to set down for a cup of coffee with him. Before I know it, I'm tellin' him about my trouble with the supervisor, and he's givin' me advice on how I can handle it. I try it too, and it works fine." He wagged his head, and winked at me. "No offense, y'know, but your dad was a real character!"

Others thought so too, though not always in a kindly way. His views, while benignly offered, were too frequently controversial. Inflation, for instance.No one else seemed to see it as a coming threat in the mid-Thirties, when he began teaching a business seminar at Rollins College. Even his colleagues thought his warning absurd. His prophecies of the black revolution and women's liberation appeared to be equally far-out, and at least once a semester, some student was likely to quit his class, calling him a damn Red. Almost as alarming to many was his adherence to Christian Science, which had, to his satisfaction, healed him of the incipient blindness that had forced him to leave Yale. Butting against the accepted limitations occupied him even in the family: he enrolled Sharlie in a course of investment at USC when she was only thirteen, taught us to type at the same time we were learning to write, and astounded us with the facts of life while most of the children we knew were still of the stork persuasion.

His revelation that sexual intercourse had a practical purpose came as a surprise to me. When I had inadvertently stumbled upon it at the age of five, I thought this interesting game was something I had personally invented, and somehow I liked it better without his explanation. More often now, I began evading his elucidation; for instance, when I was twelve and leafing through the family album. The tintype of a brooding young man caught my eye, and to my astonishment, my own name was written underneath. There had been a string of Jesse Greggs in our family over the past two hundred years, earnest deacons and merchants; but this namesake was different. He had thick black hair and a mustache like the actor who shot Lincoln. Something in his eyes searched through me, sending a sensation spangling up my spine, and I didn't want to ruin it with a reason.

As I grew up, I kept going back to the album to sneak another look at him, but only when I was fourteen, did I ask about him. "Don't know too much," my father said. "I believe he left home and was never heard of again."

"Why'd he leave home?"

"Probably afraid he would disgrace the family," he replied. "He was homosexual, I seem to have heard. Poor son of a bitch!"

My father's use of profanity was always startling. Sharlie said he only cussed so other men wouldn't think he was a prude. I don't believe he actually was a bluenose, although he was clearly in favor of the old morality. He had stayed a virgin until he married, for instance, and vainly recommended that I do the same. It was probably in the army that he had learned to camouflage his high moral standard with low jargon. "What do you mean, why?" he would demand, when I challenged his reasons for following the narrow path. "It's as plain as the nuts on a dog!"

None the less, I grew up feeling the weight of his values. I knew I wasn't going to live up to them, and wanted to avoid disappointing him when he found out. The dread of some occurrence that might expose me to him and my mother created a constant tension, a continuing need to lie. The temptation to follow the earlier Jesse and leave home grew stronger, and at last, I too fled.

Unlike my forerunner, however, I didn't disappear. I was a discreet and good son by mail, and on holidays, my parents visited me, or I came to see them. Once, after the family hadmoved away from California, we had an opportunity to return there and

The other Jess Gregg

spend August together. One of my television plays had caught the eye of a film director, and coincidentally, an aunt who wanted to travel, offered my parents her sprawling adobe house on the edge of the arroyo in Brentwood. The set-up seemed perfect for a reunion.

It should have worked. The skies were clear, the avocado trees were heavy with fruit, and on Sundays I let my father think he was teaching me how to play golf. I was careful, and kept my private life out of sight; discouraged phone calls from new friends, and although I occasionally brought one of them home late at night, I never took them into the house. A driveway lined with fir trees was ideal for my purpose, and the front seat of a car is a tradition in West Coast coupling. August was nearly over when I met a good-looking kid named Rick at an after-the-bar party, and around four in the morning, we drove into my dark driveway and parked. How long we had been there I don't know, but suddenly both of us were aware of the glimmer of a flashlight coming down the driveway toward us. Half-naked, Rick ducked to the floor of the car, and I thrust my head out the window. "Who's that?"

The quiet voice could have belonged to no one else. "Dean B."

"Well, don't come any nearer," I warned sharply.

He faltered, but kept coming, and I lost my cool entirely. *"Will you for Christ's sake go away!"* I cried.

This time he stopped. Then, without a word, he turned and went back into the house.

I drove Rick back to where he lived, and when I returned home, no one was stirring. It was getting to be daylight. Too uneasy to sleep now, I showered, changed clothes, and drove into Hollywood, dawdling over my coffee at a counter until it was time to report to my director. My mind was not on our story that day, and when I returned home after lunch, it was with the feeling that this time the showdown was inevitable. Dean B. was not around, but my mother was sitting on the terrace, and she spoke reproachfully. "There was no point in being so rude to your dad last night," she said.

"Well, why was he checking up on me?" I demanded hotly.

"But he wasn't," she defended. "He heard you drive up very late, and when you didn't come in the house, he finally began to worry you were ill—" I gave her an impatient look. "Well, it does happen," she said. "People drink too much at parties, and get sick. Even pass out."

I said, as if pushed too far, "I had a girl out there!"

She went silent, but I could tell she believed me—my excuse probably resembled all those explanations she gave herself: a son so crazy about girls, he simply couldn't decide to settle down and marry. "Well," she said abruptly, "just leave this to me, I'll see what I can do."

She was an engaging woman, with dark sympathetic eyes and prematurely white hair. No one ever tried very hard to resist her, my father least of all. She had patched up and smoothed over our tensions before, and she did so now. There were no further references to the driveway incident, and by September, when I headed back to New York, Dean B. and I appeared to be quite relaxed with each other. All the same, I don't think the breach ever really healed. Even when we joked, after that, some unspecified cross-purpose seemed to be right under the surface. My mother doubled her efforts to keep it from ever bursting back into view; but the time came when she was no longer there.

Maybe I thought a renewed understanding could still happen, because I continued going home every year at Christmas, and kept in touch with bright, carefully misrepresentative letters. On Thanksgiving, I telephoned as usual, but only Alberta was home. It would be a lively day for him, she told me—he was hosting a dinner for twelve at noon, and at five o'clock, going to the christening of a new great-granddaughter. In the meantime, he was at church, Thanksgiving being his favorite service. In his denomination, the last twenty minutes are given over to the members for brief expressions of gratitude, and Dean B., the last to get up, spoke eloquently about what life had given him. “Thank you, God,” he concluded, and sat down. Only when he failed to rise for the final hymn a few moments later did anyone realize he was gone.

“—Would we be more comfortable, having our coffee in the living room?” Sharlie was asking the lawyer.

“Could be,” he said, “but if we’re going to read the will now, it might be more convenient to sit here around the table.” He glanced from face to face, and when there was no objection, reached for his document case.

His voice, mellifluous in conversation, leveled into monotone as he began reading my father’s last wishes aloud. I listened to the dense legalese, already predicting what most of the bequests would be—provisions for his great-grandchildren’s education, a generous remembrance to Alberta for her loving care, a fund for the college. Only my own position remained obscure to me. I did not look up from my hands, but was aware of my sisters’ secret glances at me, perhaps reassuring, perhaps commiserating.

The lawyer’s voice picked up color as he came to the major bestowals, and I told myself defiantly that I didn’t care how it turned out. Still, I was holding my breath. I knew I could survive even if my father didn’t mention me at all. The hardship would be in living with the final knowledge of his rejection.

And then the lawyer’s voice said it, proof that Dean B. had shown more faith in me than I had in him. He had left his estate equally divided, bequeathing me a third of everything.

The self-reproach that shot through me then took aim again during the afternoon; while my sisters and I were going through the filing cabinets in his study, I came across an entire drawer marked with my household name, Bud. All my letters were in it, from the one I had written to him just two weeks earlier, back to the semi-suicidal scrawl from summer camp, my first time away from home. There was a gradation of snapshots of me as I grew up, most of them looking like taffy drawn out. My report cards were there too, a sheaf of drawings, an early story. Noo, glancing at my face, asked, “Why should this surprise you?”

I shook my head, unable to explain.

She resumed sorting through a pile of papers. "You two were so alike in that way, at least," she mused. "He always had trouble expressing what he felt too. Not what he thought, but what he *felt.*"

She got to talking about those months after our mother died, when he just sat there, day after day, neatly dressed and unfailingly polite, laying out spreads of double solitaire on the dining table. Then suddenly, he had snapped out of it—broke through that barrier of reserve that had constrained him all his life. "I suddenly realized that whatever I missed in your mother, I myself could be," he told Noo. "That wonderful enthusiasm of hers—-when I missed it, *I* could be it. Her warmth and thoughtfulness: *I* could be warm and thoughtful. Her humor, her imagination, her sympathy. I could be all these qualities, and she would exist *in* me, *as* me."

The thought that swept through me surprised me: *I wish I had known that man!*

That same thought came to me a day later, and then frequently. During the month it took my sisters and me to sort through the house and close it up, I finally began to read him. It was such a rich time, I was sorry to bring it to an end, but I had left someone in New York, and it was time to get back to him. There was no possible way to explain this to Sharlie and Noo so I told them I had to get back to my work. Only as I was packing my suitcase did it occur to me that this was the excuse I had always used to keep my father from knowing too much about me. "Sorry I can't talk now, Dean B., I've got to get back to work." "Love to see you, Dad, but I can't leave my work just now."

Yet why such secrecy had seemed so important to me, I could no longer explain. This man I had begun to know surely would have found some understanding for me too. It even seemed probable he had known all about me anyway, and had waited with tact and forbearance for some indication that it was all right to acknowledge it.

A suspicion began to sneak up on me that, in all my life, I had never been myself with the people who meant the most to me. I had kept them strangers, and myself a stranger to them. And worse, I was intending to go on doing this as long as I lived. The alternative was just too risky. If I confessed I was gay to Noo, the gentler of my sisters, she might understand—but suppose she didn't? Suppose I saw hurt in her eyes, or distaste? And Sharlie, closest friend of my childhood—could I spare her now if she turned away? I knew I couldn't; felt again, as I had felt my whole life, that secrecy was safer, at least with the family.

Shutting my suitcase, I went downstairs. Yet as I passed Dean B.'s study, empty now except for packing crates, I suddenly knew how he would react to my cautious reasoning. "*Balls!*" he would say. And for that moment, anyway, I knew I had them. I could hear the murmur of my sisters chatting on the screen porch, waiting to drive me to the airport. I glanced at my watch. There was time, and I set down my suitcase. "Hey, girls," I called, hearing Dean B.'s inflection in my voice, "would you step into the office—?"

## - 21 -

## LO

A glance at each other as we passed on the street was introduction enough. I looked back at him, and he was looking back at me, a tall kid with big shoulders and wide, gentle eyes. His light brown hair wasn't forever, but his complexion was fresh and his mouth vividly red. Twenty-two or twenty-three years old, I judged—-far too young for me. In my forties now, I was a lot more comfortable with tricks nearer my own age.

I walked on. I started to anyway, but the image of those shoulders and that coloring forced me to look back again. His smile

Lo

was direct and boyish. I hesitated, but a moment later, we were walking side by side. As we reached my door, I spoke for the first time. "Like to come up?"

"All right."

It was our last conversation for an hour, maybe two—time doesn't register in bed. "I've got to get along," he finally said. But he kept turning back to study a tattered old French poster I had pinned to my wall. "Like it?" I asked. He nodded, and correctly identified the graceful dancer pictured there: Cleo de Merode. "How did you know that?" I demanded.

"Because she posed for Degas and Lautrec," he said. "And I'm an artist too." He beamed like some patriot promoting his homeland: "An impressionist."

I showed him my other posters from that era—the writer, Colette, skimming along like an ice skater, the heartless Otero flinging about in all her jewels, and a dazzling mid-air celebration of cough lozenges by Cheret. We swapped the kind of story that collectors torment themselves with—once I had allowed fifty dollars to stand between me and a torn, but genuine Lautrec poster; once, he had had a chance to buy a color etching by Mary Cassatt for next to nothing, and let it get away. We discovered other interests in common too, and found that we laughed at the same sort of thing. Both of us were surprised to notice it had gotten dark outside. I suggested we have some dinner at a nearby pasta place, and later walked him to his digs down near the Holland Tunnel. A tiny warren of rooms in a crumbling brick building served as his studio, bunkhouse, and catch-all. The furniture was old, crowded together and nearly buried under clothes, art supplies, and great billowing plants. Everywhere I turned there were paintings, raw and unframed—orchards, sky-drifts, flowering hillsides. I particularly liked a chalk drawing of red and purple anemones, and he gave it to me.

We saw each other the next day. The next one too. One evening, he brought over some Asti Spumante, and we drank it warm out of the bottle, sitting up in bed. I didn't get tight, or even high, yet somehow felt intoxicated. I was doing research for a prison novel, *Baby Boy*, and never let anything interfere with my schedule; just the same, we went to a movie the next afternoon, and the following Saturday, spent five hours together at an art museum. I discovered he knew the names of all birds, all trees, and all the supporting players in old films—-Olga Baclanova, Guy Kibbee, Wynne Gibson, performers I thought only I remembered. In the third week, he phoned at four in the morning, burning up with fever, and I rushed downtown to take care of him. I wondered if I were getting too involved. I loved being with Lo, as I called him, and was flattered by his continued interest in me, but I was wary. To admire youth was one thing, but to entrust my happiness to it, quite another. Fortunately, I was scheduled to go to Portugal a week later, and felt sure that by the time I returned, my balance would be restored.

The loneliness I had almost forgotten about that previous month with Lo met me at Lisbon. I tried to counteract it at the beach at Capricos, whose convoluted paths in the underbrush made it the most welcoming stretch of sand this side of Fire Island; but the flood-tide of adventure there only seemed to exacerbate the feeling of isolation. I became more than ever aware of how much of my life was spent with people I only met once.

An unexpected mirror in the cabana startled me into seeing myself as a stranger might: interesting eyes, but a much lived-in face. I was still slim, and thanks to my constancy at the gym, my pecs and biceps were sharply defined; but to hold the interest of one so much younger, I would need a lot more than any mirror could reflect—things like patience, good humor, fidelity, and, probably, forgiveness. My record here was poor. None of my love affairs had lasted very long. My attention span was brief, and my temper, quick. Disappointment in my career had sharpened my tongue until a pal of mine, Joe, conjectured that it must make kissing a hazard.

Suddenly, I was scribbling all these negatives down in a letter, warning Lo in advance, utterly frank about everything except that I had a police record. I mailed it off before I could become rational again, and retracted it a hundred times in my head before his reply finally followed me to Paris. Even as I unfolded the letter, I assumed the worst from its formality—he had signed it with his full name the way people do complaints about a neighbor's dog. However, the message itself restored my hope. Come home, it said. And at the bottom of the page, beneath that serious signature, "I burned your letter, in case you ever become famous."

Not immediately, but soon after my return, he moved into my little apartment on University Place. Very quickly, it lost its identity as mine, and became a painting-packed, clothes-littered replica of his Holland Tunnel studio, even to the smell of turpentine and garlic bread. I had never learned to cook—for years, had gone out for meals three times a day—but Lo brought several pots and pans with him, converted the tiny bathroom into a kitchen, and managed to cook three-course dinners on a hot plate. Of course, we had to turn off most of the lights while the food heated up, so as not to overwhelm my one-fuse electrical circuit; but the regular meals finally began to hide my hollows.

My friends all met Lo and liked him, but not even Joe, the most positive person I knew, expected this affair to last: being faithful to one person was still an experiment for me. We were still together by summer, however, and on week-ends, went out to the Hamptons and stayed with Marion Cole. Lo loved it there—the motionless golden light by day, the nearness of the stars at night, and always the sea. Winslow Homer had once painted these dunes and windmills, he told me. So had Childe Hassam and William Merritt Chase. I got used to him suddenly forgetting everything else, and, squinting at the distances, making quick mental sketches. The only cloud on this horizon was the strain of being at Marion's. Some of the other boys staying there seemed attracted to Lo too, keeping me apprehensive and over-vigilant. And Marion, herself, appeared to be different:

carping, even resentful. We began looking around for another place.

The alternatives were murderously expensive. "Even garage apartments seem to be priced by the ounce," I complained to a gentlewoman I knew. She started to apologize, as if it were all her fault. "Although," she added thoughtfully, "I have a— Well, you wouldn't be interested, it's so—" The flutter of her hands tried to say it. So did the embarrassment in her eyes. To prove what couldn't be articulated, she walked us to the back of her estate, and let us see for ourselves. Hidden from the road by overgrown shrubs was a strange little structure in a state of serious disrepair. The roof sagged, the remaining paint had crackled into mosaic, and grass grew in the rain gutters. It had been the carriage house in more splendid times, but since then, and for reasons she never explained, the stable, gazebo, and chicken coop had been moved up and tacked on to it, making an oddly joined complex of rooms. It was, in short, so ideal for us, we could scarcely keep a look of disdain on our faces as we bargained for it. I suggested that in lieu of rent for the next three months, Lo and I repair this—this— I searched for words sufficiently depreciating—this *pathetic* ruin. Our hostess, a bullet-proof powder puff if there ever was one, adored the idea of us making it habitable again, but fixed a good round sum for the privilege. "*And*," she added, with logic that was all her own,"for fifty dollars *more*, you can stay through the winter for nothing."

It is true that the little house was not winterized—there was no heat or insulation, and the inside walls were made of thin cardboard. However, there was electricity and running water, and the roof only leaked badly in one area. Buying a bucket, some house paint, and a small Franklin stove, we moved in before reason could take control.

It was a new kind of life for us both. We were up in the mornings at six to get in some writing or painting before we had to resume the home repairs that, each day, outclassed our ingenuity. Afternoons were spent swimming in the surf, and evenings, dancing at the gay discos. By the end of the first month, we dropped the discos as not really conducive to keeping a new couple together. We were both eager to leave the Quicksilver Mine, as we called the underground life—fast-moving, mercurial, but finally lethal. To cement the feeling of family, we decided to get a dog, and learned of a male Sheltie whose present owners were about to divorce. As neither of them wanted the other to have him, their solution was to give him away to strangers. We phoned at once, and asked to be considered.

I had owned a Sheltie before, a perky gold and white winner. However, gold, white and perky was not what was led up to our door that night. The poor animal clearly knew he was being given away—his eyes were despairing, his tail drooped, and worry had thinned his coat. Only Picasso could have admired his gray and black markings, or understood the thin white line that divided his face, separating the spots on one side from the stripes on the other. His name was Toby, and his papers argued that he was thoroughbred, but although Lo was willing to accept him, I held out for more lively, not to mention better looking, companionship. Deciding to return him to his owners in the morning, I fixed him a bed in the corner. His mournful eyes followed me wherever I went, reminding me of times I had not pleased either. As I bent down to commiserate with him, he suddenly reached up and licked me across the face. There was no question after that—we had a dog!

Other matters were not so immediately resolved. The corporation that Lo worked for moved to Washington, and offered to relocate him there at a better salary. Although he made his choice to stay on with me and Toby, the new work he found was unrewarding. What he really longed to do now was try his luck as a full-time artist, but since his savings were modest, and he would take no help from me, that would have to wait on developments. These came, but at their own speed, and by ways so labyrinthine as to be almost invisible. In my third year with him, the real estate office that had become our landlord in the city began making loud noises about the amount of time we were spending out on Long Island. There were new housing restrictions, my lawyer told me "—and in the end they'll force you out of the apartment on University Place," he added. "Still, that could take a couple of years, so it might be worth the company's time to make you a generous offer to clear out sooner."

Clear out we did, the following summer. The cash settlement helped us find a gallery-like store front in the Hamptons, and, serving suitable wine and cheese, we exhibited a whole spectrum of paintings Lo had done of Long Island's south fork. One of the critics called them "overtly picturesque," utter damnation in that time of abstract expressionism; but he sold six landscapes, enough to launch his career as a painter. However, leaving University Place left us no place to live now but my father's home in Florida, and the carriage house on the Island, a building no sturdier than a stage set, and with winter always waiting in the wings.

No, it was not entirely comfortable there, yet we came back to it year after year, arriving just after the first crocus, and leaving again only when the water began to freeze in the vases. Our benign rent inevitably escalated, but so, amazingly, did our combined incomes. We joined a local church, supported the library fund, and got to know our neighbors. The ivy we planted took over the fence, and a maple sapling by the front door gradually became a tree. Lo and I began to sound like each other, the way old couples do; and like them, we slammed doors and shouted at each other once or twice a year. Both of us still remember when, for the third time, he served ratatouille, a dish he knew I hated, and I threw it out into the garden. He knocked me down. I broke a flower pot over his head. Somehow, our future survived it.

More and more, that was on our minds—surviving. It did not always seem possible. We had been shocked when one of our friends died after what seemed little more than a fever. He was only in his thirties, and people didn't die that young. Then another died. And another. Nobody spoke of anything else, and suddenly we realized we were in the center of a plague. Its very name seemed to mock us: it was no aid to our newfound freedom. No cure for it was known, and the only precaution Lo and I could think of was to withdraw still further into our tight little world, population two.

It seemed the perfect solution to everything, except that my work stopped. Back some years—about the time we got our cardboard house really fit to live in—I had sold a novel to Hollywood, and put a payment down on a place of our own. However, this added security did not prepare me for the months that followed when I sat down to write every morning, and not a word occurred to me. I had been happier these past years than ever before in my life, yet somehow the words, the images, the meaning, had stopped.

"Did you think that isolating yourself from the world wouldn't have a cost?" my friend Joe asked.

Joe was the only one of my old New York circle who would brave the rattle and grime of the Long Island Railroad to come out to visit. In fact, he had completed his first book in the shed that we liked to think of as our guestroom. "Downtown Joe," he was affectionately called, or sometimes, "Saint Joe," for he was devout. Vigorous, vivacious, unshakable in his convictions, looking like a pocket-edition of Mark Twain, he gathered signatures for worthy causes, served at soup kitchens, nursed the plague-stricken, and, from the first moment of the Stonewall Rebellion, joined a group of writers and thinkers in marching towards freedom.

His accusation infuriated me. "What do you mean, *isolating myself from the world?"* I demanded.

"What else do you call it?" he asked. His gesture withered the garden we were sitting in: "You've hidden yourself a hundred miles outside of this century."

"Having a few fucking hollyhocks doesn't mean I'm out of touch with the world," I protested.

Even after Joe had taken the train back to New York, his accusation remained. I stormed along the beach, kicking up the sand and sometimes hurling chunks of driftwood back into the waves. How could he say I'd hidden myself from the world? It was true I seldom got into the city anymore, but after all, what were telephones for? And if I no longer subscribed to a morning paper, I faithfully *watched* the news every evening. Yet despite my skill and practice in evading the issue, there was not a minute when I didn't know exactly what he had been talking about. The battle for gay liberation was going on outside my garden wall, and I was no part of it. I had lost friends to AIDS, but my response to this was limited to regret. A whole new point of view was forming in the world, and I, while out of the closet, was still watching from the bedroom. "You were asking why you've stopped writing," Joe had said just before he boarded the train. "I'm suggesting it's because you have nothing to say anymore. You've settled for contentment."

When I returned home, Lo asked, "Did Joe have any suggestions?"

I faked innocence. "About what?"

"What to do about your writer's block."

"Nothing that would be of any help to me," I mumbled.

However, Joe's impassioned words came back every time I sat down and tried to write. I did not even make notes to myself now, but simply stared at that terrible foolscap Sahara. The only image that came to my mind was of an amputee wincing at the pain in a limb that wasn't there anymore.

And Lo kept coming up with solutions. "Suppose," he said, that night, "just suppose that, instead of thinking you have to make up stories and invent characters, you were to simply *report*? Maybe tell about some of the shit you had to put up with, back in the bad old days?"

Those bad old days were something he and I had never talked about, and the coolness of my voice was meant to discourage our starting to now. "Tell about it to what purpose?" I asked.

He spoke as if this were something he had thought about for a long time: a generation of kids was coming out now who had no idea how tough things used to be for gay people, he said.

They thought it had always been as easy-going as it was today, "—and that it 'll automatically go on this way all by itself."

I escaped into the dark garden, but he followed after me. "And that leaves them unguarded," he persisted, "because the opposition hasn't gone away, and all the old injustices could gradually sneak back—"

I had enough problems without going back to those memories, I told him. "And even if I wanted to, the words don't oblige anymore."

It was around four that morning when I woke up and was unable to get back to sleep. So as not to waken Lo, I sneaked into our other room and tried to read; tried watching TV too, and even meditating, but nothing helped. Instead, I kept getting feelings I didn't want, the old uneasiness, the isolation, the anger. It was only June, and the windows were open, yet I was sweating. I saw the glitter of lights, and the reflection of a smile in a plate glass window. I heard the husky decoy speak enticingly, and when I responded, glimpsed the flash of brass in his wallet as he told me I was under arrest.

*Make it work for you*, Agnes had told me—*anger, failure, shame!* I hushed her voice, but there were others now, even my own. Suddenly whole phrases were coming out of me like the gush from a wound. I wasn't prepared for them—had no paper handy, and in this exigency, was forced to scrawl the words down on whatever I could find, the fly leaf of a book, the margins of a page, the backs of old telephone messages. Eventually, there was a wild scatter of makeshift manuscript around my chair. I was exhausted, and at the same time, too keyed up to rest. Hardly knowing what I would find, I gathered the papers up from the floor.

The writing was scarcely legible and not always coherent. At times, it seemed to be the outcry of someone I scarcely knew, and for a moment, I was tempted to hide or destroy it. Instead, I hunted up some foolscap and began to copy my scrawl onto clean sheets of paper, writing each word clearly this time.

By the time I had finished, daylight was coming in the windows, and I could hear Lo calling sleepily from the next room. I didn't answer yet, but glanced back at the copy. "*Hollywood Boulevard was crowded, but nobody seemed to be going anywhere,*" it began. "*The tourists drifted aimlessly, and so did I, until I noticed that one of them was cruising me—*"

I was out at last.

## Acknowledgements

My many thanks to Elise D'Haene, my editor, and to Martin and Judy Shepard of the Permanent Press. I'm also grateful for the wonderful support of Julie Fallowfield, Victoria Hartman, John Laudando, Leo Revi, Laura Stein, Neenyah Ostrom, and Richard Philp. Sherry Ogilvie and Jenelle Bailey too. Credit Alan Einhorn for patience and skill when I had to be photographed. And thanks to Blossom Akst Levy for giving me permission to use lyrics from her Dad's song, *Am I Blue?*

Some of this material has appeared in a different form in *Christopher Street*, *Dance Magazine*, and *Readers Digest*.